W9-AUQ-894

INTENTIONAL TALK

HOW TO STRUCTURE AND LEAD PRODUCTIVE MATHEMATICAL DISCUSSIONS

Stenhouse Publishers
Portland, Maine

ELHAM KAZEMI & ALLISON HINTZ

Foreword by Megan Franke

Stenhouse Publishers
www.stenhouse.com

Copyright © 2014 by Elham Kazemi and Allison Hintz

All rights reserved. Except for the pages in the appendix, which may be photocopied for classroom use, no part of this publication may be reproduced or transmitted in any form or by any means, electronic or mechanical, including photocopy, or any information storage and retrieval system, without permission from the publisher.

Every effort has been made to contact copyright holders and students for permission to reproduce borrowed material. We regret any oversights that may have occurred and will be pleased to rectify them in subsequent reprints of the work.

Library of Congress Cataloging-in-Publication Data
Kazemi, Elham, 1970– author.
Intentional talk : how to structure and lead productive mathematical discussions / Elham Kazemi and Allison Hintz ; foreword by Megan Franke.
pages cm
Includes bibliographical references and index.
ISBN 978-1-57110-976-7 (pbk. : alk. paper)—ISBN 978-1-62531-008-8 (ebook) 1. Forums (Discussion and debate) 2. Mathematics—Study and teaching (Elementary) 3. Problem solving—Study and teaching (Elementary) I. Hintz, Allison, 1962– author. II. Title.
QA20.F67K39 2014
372.7—dc23

2013040033

Cover design, interior design, and typesetting by Martha Drury

Manufactured in the United States of America

PRINTED ON 30% PCW
RECYCLED PAPER

20 19 18 17 16 15 9 8 7 6 5 4

For Grace, Neeku, Roshann, and William

CONTENTS

FOREWORD

By Megan Franke

Elham Kazemi and Allison Hintz take you inside mathematics classrooms and highlight the details of practice that will help you create productive mathematics discussions in your own classroom. Whether you are a teacher new to mathematics conversations or have been enjoying them with your students for a long time, *Intentional Talk* will speak to you. Elham and Allison provide vignettes, a set of principles to guide your decision making, and a collection of tools to help you navigate this complex work. This combination will help you develop your vision of what is possible, know how to improve what you are doing now, and continue to learn and improve your practice.

Everything we know about student learning and classroom practice tells us that classroom conversations are crucial to mathematics learning. We know that students who explain the details of their mathematical ideas, engage with the details of others' mathematical ideas, and have others engage with their own mathematical ideas achieve mathematically. We also know that engaging in mathematical conversations in productive ways can help students see themselves as smart and competent in mathematics. We have seen that students who take part in mathematical conversations also learn to listen to others, ask insightful and respectful questions, and reflect on their own understandings. For these reasons and more, we must make the most of and continually improve our classroom mathematics discussions.

We know that orchestrating classroom discussions can be challenging. Elham and Allison build on all of the wonderful and productive classroom discussion work and detail what it looks and feels like to navigate the moment-to-moment interactions within mathematics classroom discussions. They tease out the different types of mathematical conversations that can occur. They share ways to design and carry out strategy-sharing conversations as well as a range of more targeted talk. The principles and tools provided for each kind of discussion will guide you toward meeting your mathematical goals as well as the needs of each and every one of your students.

Intentional Talk will help you create a classroom where all of your students are engaged in mathematical discussions in ways that help them learn and see themselves as mathematicians. You will want to read it more than once; you will want to mark pages, copy the tools, and revisit the student and teacher interactions often.

ACKNOWLEDGMENTS

This book has been in the making for more than ten years, and we owe many thanks to Toby Gordon, our amazing editor at Stenhouse, for sparking the idea of a book on classroom discussions many moons ago and for being there to see this project to fruition. Her encouragement and guidance helped us see this work to the finish line. We were also helped by the ideas of two anonymous reviewers, who took great care in giving us feedback to strengthen our drafts. Adrian Cunard, Becca Lewis, and Teresa Lind were kind enough to read and provide helpful comments on early drafts.

We give special thanks to the staff and students at Lakeridge Elementary School in Renton, Washington, who fill these pages with their brilliant ideas. It has been a life-changing experience working with you. Thank you for opening your classrooms and being willing to take risks, try new ideas, and teach us so much about cultivating rich classroom communities that nurture children's minds as well as their humanity. A special thank-you to photographer Matt Hagen for capturing the beautiful images of Lakeridge teachers and students used throughout the book and to Lynsey Gibbons and Kendra Lomax for organizing the photographs.

We have learned so much from the scholarship and practice of many others in the field of mathematics and teacher education. It is difficult to convey how much we are indebted to the team of scholars and teachers that have contributed to the development of Cognitively Guided Instruction (CGI): researchers Tom Carpenter, Elizabeth Fennema, Megan Franke, Linda Levi, Susan Empson, Randy Philipp, and Vicki Jacobs; and the CGI teachers from Madison, Wisconsin, especially Annie Keith and Mazie Jenkins. We believe that children's mathematical thinking is at the heart of inspired teaching. Megan Franke, thank you for everything. We stand in awe of you. The principles that have guided our work derive from our collaboration with Megan and other members of the Learning in, from, and for Teaching Practice (LTP) group:

Magdalene Lampert, Hala Ghousseini, Heather Beasley, Kate Crowe, Adrian Cunard, and Angela Turrou. We are grateful for the way the LTP group challenged us to bring to life the important work teachers do when leading mathematical discussions. We have benefited from collaboration with our colleagues in the Mathematics Education Project (MEP) at the University of Washington and the Expanding the Community of Mathematics Learners (ECML) project, where we, Allison and Elham, met. So many of our ideas about designing professional learning experiences and working with teachers have emerged from the energetic and thoughtful ideas of our MEP and ECML colleagues: Julia Aguirre, Ruth Balf, Filiberto Barajas-López, Sunshine Campbell, Lisa Jilk, Megan Kelley-Petersen, Anita Lenges, Laura Mah, Leslie Nielsen, Katy Pence, Rosemary Sheffield, Gini Stimpson, and Bryan Street. These are just a few of the hundreds of teachers and teacher educators with whom we have worked who have dedicated themselves to improving their practice, digging deeply into content together, and transforming the mathematical learning experiences of children.

Our knowledge about teaching and discourse has been greatly informed by the inspirational work of many other scholars and their teaching and research teams: Deborah Ball, Virginia Bastable, Jo Boaler, Courtney Cazden, Suzanne Chapin, Marta Civil, Paul Cobb, Maarten Dolk, Cathy Fosnot, Karen Fuson, Kim Hufferd-Ackles, Cathy Humphries, Magdalene Lampert, Kay McClain, Sarah Michaels, Judit Moschkovich, Catherine O'Connor, Mike Rose, Susan Jo Russell, Deborah Schifter, Peg Smith, Mary Kay Stein, Terry Wood, and Erna Yackel.

Our families have been a source of love, strength, patience, and laughter. Abolghassem and Nahid, thank you for your many sacrifices, love, and wisdom. Mark, Roshann, and Neeku, you are always and forever a source of joy and light and adventure. Mrs. P., thank you for your steadfast love, kindness, and generosity. Becky and Ken, or "Mimi and Papa," thank you for your generous gift of time and loving support. Shawn, Grace, and William, you are treasures and a constant source of inspiration.

CHAPTER 1

INTRODUCTION

Leading mathematical discussions can be both invigorating and challenging. It's easy to start a discussion by asking children to share their thinking. And nothing beats those moments when children proudly share something they figured out. But then what? Math discussions aren't just about show-and-tell: stand up, sit down, clap, clap, clap. Knowing what to do with students' ideas and teaching children how to meaningfully participate in discussions can be a lot more daunting.

We often worry during a discussion that students might get lost trying to keep up with what everyone is saying or that they may simply tune out when a lot of ideas are shared. And no teacher likes that uncomfortable feeling of putting a child on the spot. Yet when teachers plan for and steer productive discussions, children realize it's worth listening to one another and that it's okay to be pressed to say more.

Not all mathematical discussions have the same aim or should be led in the same way. In this book, we describe how considering your goals for math talk can help you better design discussions to meet those goals and teach children to participate meaningfully.

Our work with classroom discussions is guided by four principles:

1. Discussions should achieve a mathematical goal, and different types of goals require planning and leading discussions differently.
2. Students need to know what and how to share so their ideas are heard and are useful to others.
3. Teachers need to orient students to one another and the mathematical ideas so that every member of the class is involved in achieving the mathematical goal.
4. Teachers must communicate that all children are sense makers and that their ideas are valued.

These principles are at the heart of creating classrooms where children can participate equitably. Sarah Michaels, Mary Catherine O'Connor, and Megan Williams Hall (2010) write about classroom communities that live by these principles as engaging in "accountable talk," or "talk that seriously responds to and further develops what others in the group have said" (1). The challenge, of course, lies in putting these principles into action, which is what we hope to help you do.

The classroom vignettes in this book reflect insights we have gained into leading mathematical discussions while working closely with teachers who are committed to equity in students' achievements and learning opportunities. These vignettes are inspired by the way these teachers are creating practices to challenge school structures that sort and label children according to ability. We hope the everyday brilliance of the teachers and children in these pages will help us all strive toward creating classrooms that disrupt longstanding assumptions about who can and cannot excel in mathematics (Delpit 2012).

We'll now say a bit more about what we mean by each of these principles, give you a glimpse into the ways particular mathematical goals can help you run a discussion, and then outline what lies ahead in the rest of this book.

Principle 1: Discussions Should Achieve a Mathematical Goal

The mathematical goal acts as your compass as you navigate classroom talk. The goal helps you decide what to listen for, which ideas to pursue, and which to highlight. In *5 Practices for Orchestrating Productive Mathematics Discussions* (2011), Margaret Smith and Mary Kay Stein describe the importance of teachers clearly specifying the mathematical goal before planning out a discussion. The mathematical ideas at the heart of a lesson will help you distinguish between different types of classroom discussions you can have with your students.

Sometimes your aim is to have students share as many different ideas as possible in the discussion so they see a range of possibilities. We call this "open strategy sharing," because we're working on building students' repertoire of strategies. The class generates lots of ideas, and the discussion likely moves across a broad terrain that includes mathematical concepts, procedures, representations, and explanations (see Figure 1.1). Students listen for and contribute different ways to solve the same problem.

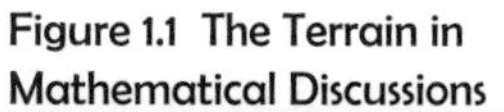
Figure 1.1 The Terrain in Mathematical Discussions

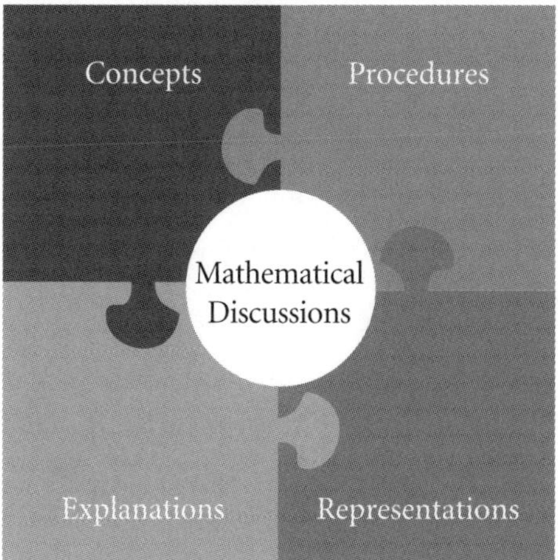

At other times you might want to focus the discussion on a particular idea. We call this "targeted discussion." Through targeted sharing the discussion zooms in on a particular idea. This more focused sharing involves specific goals, like defining and using key terms or concepts correctly, revising an incorrect strategy, or making sense of a particular representation. The students listen to and contribute ideas in order to move toward consensus. The table below lists the targeted discussion structures that will be the focus of Chapters 3 through 7.

Targeted Discussion Structure	Goal
Compare and Connect	to compare similarities and differences among strategies
Why? Let's Justify	to generate justifications for why a particular mathematical strategy works
What's Best and Why?	to determine a best (most efficient) solution strategy in a particular circumstance
Define and Clarify	to define and discuss appropriate ways to use mathematical models, tools, vocabulary, or notation
Troubleshoot and Revise	to reason through which strategy produces a correct solution or figure out where a strategy went awry

Principle 2: Students Need to Know What and How to Share

To make classroom discussions come alive, students need help knowing how to participate. When students have the chance to express their ideas, teachers have more information about what students *do* understand, what they are grappling with, and where they might be stumbling or confused. Students learn through classroom discussions *what* to share. In this book, we provide guidance for how to structure each type of discussion. We also pay attention to how students learn to contribute meaningfully in different types of discussions. We need to provide clear models for what an explanation sounds like and we need to judge, based on learning goals for students, what mathematical ideas require an explanation at any particular time. Students learn what to share as we prompt them to articulate important parts of their explanations. We can use and offer sentence starters that cue students to know what to say: "Explain to me what you meant by ______," "What would you do if the number was ______?" and "How is your way different from ______?" We also help students learn what to listen for so they can contribute to the conversation: "Listen for how she broke apart the numbers," "Think about whether you are understanding how she used the number line to show her thinking."

Similarly, students learn *how* to share through our explicit support. Reinforcing norms supports students in knowing how to share. For example, you might need to reinforce where to place oneself ("Stand here so we can see your work"); how loudly to speak ("Speak loudly so everyone can hear your idea"); and what tools to use ("Use the drawing in your journal to help"). We want to help children crack the code of being successful in meaningful mathematical learning at the same time that we tap into and draw on the resources they bring to the classroom (Aguirre, Mayfield-Ingram, and Martin 2013).

Principle 3: Teachers Need to Orient Students to One Another and the Mathematical Ideas

One of the challenges of leading discussions is bringing the whole class into the discussion. Most classrooms have several students who are eager to share and will always raise their hands and volunteer their thoughts. If we always call on these students, it's easy for others to remain passive or become anxious about how to enter the discussion. But that's not the only problem; if students have their hands raised just to get in their two cents, you'll end up with a bunch of ideas that don't build on each other or go anywhere. Teachers have to use strategies that help students learn *how* to attend to each other's ideas and the mathematics. We call this orienting students to one another and the mathematics. Teachers can draw attention to the meaningful contributions that all students make and can encourage students to take risks by "assigning competence," or identifying and naming students' specific contributions (Featherstone et al. 2011). The vignettes in this book will demonstrate many different ways that teachers advance the mathematical agenda of a discussion by strategically highlighting a student's insight or contribution, especially when a student might not be feeling confident about his or her standing with the rest of the class.

Principle 4: Teachers Must Communicate That All Students Are Sense Makers and That Their Ideas Are Valued

Our last principle is also the most important principle to put into action, because children have to be willing to take risks and put their ideas out there. Discussions obviously open up the possibilities that students will share their partial and incorrect understandings. How we respond to errors and partially developed ideas sends important messages about taking risks. It is not easy for students to express their ideas if there is a high burden to be correct and understand everything the first time around.

We need to remember that there's always a logic behind why students think the way they do, even if they seem off base. We also need to recognize publicly students' ideas, making sure we don't single out just a few students as mathematically "smart." There are many ways to be smart in mathematics, including making connections across ideas, representing problems, working with models, figuring out faulty solutions, finding patterns, making conjectures, persisting with challenging problems, working through errors, and searching for efficient solutions (Featherstone et al. 2011). Being smart in mathematics is not just about speed and accuracy. Vivian Paley writes that being curious about children's ideas signals to them that they are respected: "What are these ideas that I have that are *so* interesting to the teacher? I must be somebody with good ideas" (1986, 127). We want all students in the class to regard themselves as mathematical thinkers and to see themselves as people who can grow and be successful.

So how do these principles come together in teacher-led discussions? Let's consider two examples, an open strategy share and two types of targeted discussions, to see these principles in action.

Open Strategy Sharing: The Case of Mental Math

You might already have some experience leading discussions that fall into our open strategy sharing category. Discussing mental math strategies is a good example of open strategy sharing. It is a routine practice in elementary mathematics classrooms and is designed to build children's ability to flexibly, efficiently, and accurately compute. The teacher starts by posing a computational problem, such as 5 + 2, 12 – 7, 21 × 4, or 96 ÷ 6, and invites children to share the different ways they figured out the answer.

Ms. Lind picks a multiplication problem for her fourth graders to solve as a warm-up to her main lesson. She's expecting to have the students spend about ten minutes sharing a few different ways of solving the problem. After writing 25 × 18 on the board, she steps to the side and provides time for her students to solve this problem mentally. As she sees that children have arrived at their solutions, she whispers to them to write their strategies in their math journals (she hopes this will help students remember the steps of their strategies). She circulates through the room, noticing the ways that students have approached the problem. When it looks like everyone has at least one solution, she asks the students to call out together what they got for the product. She records their ideas on the board to help make sure she doesn't put any one child on the spot to be correct or incorrect and to give herself the chance to see if there are multiple ideas in the room. She hears two different answers, 498 and 450. With all the ideas out, she begins by calling on a child who she could see has used a strategy that's fairly common in the class. Ms. Lind knows that asking Faduma to use her notebook will help her feel more comfortable sharing.

Ms. Lind: Okay, Faduma, tell us about what you wrote as you figured out this solution. I want everyone else to think about whether you are understanding what Faduma did and if you used a similar or different strategy.

Ms. Lind's opening words help students know what to share and invite listeners into the discussion. She tries to help them know what to listen for.

Faduma: Since I can multiply numbers by 10, I broke up the 18 to a 10 and an 8. I multiplied 25 times 10 and 25 times 8. I got 250 plus 200, which is 450.

Ms. Lind: Thank you.

As Ms. Lind records Faduma's solution on the board, she notices that many students signal that they used the same strategy with the sign for "me too," inspired by the sign from American Sign Language. Children make the sign with one hand near their chest (or even close to their head), folding over their three middle fingers and rocking their hand back and forth (Parrish 2010; see Figure 1.2).

Figure 1.2 Students show the sign for "me too."

Ms. Lind: I've written on the board what I heard Faduma say. And many of you are showing me that you did the same thing. Who can add on to help us explain why we would split the eighteen the way Faduma did?

This question reinforces Ms. Lind's cue for listeners to see if they understand Faduma's ideas, which she gave at the beginning of the discussion.

Jordan: Well, it's like Faduma said, multiplying by 10 can be easier to do. So since one way of thinking about 25 times 18 is that you have 25 18 times, you can first do 25 10 times and then you have 8 more 25s.

Students signal agreement with Jordan. And Ms. Lind adds some words to what she has recorded to help make this explanation visible in the class display (see Figure 1.3).

Figure 1.3 Faduma's Strategy

25 × 18 = 450 (this means 25 18 times)

25 × 10 = 250 (this means 25 10 times)
25 × 8 = 200 (this means 25 8 times)

Ms. Lind: Does anyone have a question for Faduma?

Marcus: I do. I kind of solved it the same way but I got a different answer. Eighteen is close to 20 so I did 20 times 25 to get 500, but then I subtracted 2 to get to 498. I'm not sure why our answers are different.

Ms. Lind records Marcus's strategy on the board (Figure 1.4) to display for others what he is saying. She already begins to wonder whether she should pursue his question now or wait for another discussion.

Figure 1.4 Marcus's Strategy and Question

$25 \times 18 = \square$
$25 \times 20 = 500$
$500 - 2 = 498$

Marcus: Why is this answer different from Faduma's?

Ms. Lind: So you're really trying to make sense of Faduma's strategy through your own way. I'm writing your question up here, but before we take up your question, let's see if we can put one more strategy up here and maybe that will help us think about what is going on.

Ms. Lind makes this move given her goal of eliciting a range of ways to solve the problem. She also knows that Marcus's strategy, trying to round up and compensate for the difference, is not yet widespread in the class and may need some special attention.

Celia: *(Raising her hand to add to the discussion.)* I used what I know about quarters. Four quarters make one dollar. So 16 make 400 and then 2 more make 450.

Ms. Lind: *(Orienting the class to Celia.)* Celia, you gave us a lot to think about. What do you think Celia means when she says that quarters helped her solve the problem? And if you're not sure, you can ask her to repeat what she said.

Ms. Lind invites other students to be responsible for making sense of Celia's idea. She reinforces the idea that it's okay to ask Celia to share her idea again. Encouraging repetition gets several students to explain that Celia is thinking about the problem as 18 quarters, because quarters are worth 25 cents. Since 4 quarters make 1 dollar, Celia is thinking about 4 groups of 25 at a time. Ms. Lind puts Celia in the role of confirming or clarifying what her classmates say until they understand what Celia did. Ms. Lind writes Celia's strategy on the board (Figure 1.5).

Ms. Lind: *(Prompting students to think about the strategies shared so far.)* We seem to have three different strategies and two different answers. Could you turn and talk to your elbow partner about which strategies convince you and what questions you have?

Figure 1.5 Celia's Strategy

25 × 18 is like 18 quarters
Every 4 quarters is $1.00
So every 4 25s is 100
4 × 25 = 100
18 can be broken up into 4 + 4 + 4 + 4 + 2
100 + 100 + 100 + 100 + 50 = 450

This partner talk allows students to process what they have heard and gives Ms. Lind the chance to monitor the pairs and potentially select a few ideas to close out the discussion for the day.

Ms. Lind: I'm noticing as I listen to you that you are thinking about how your classmates broke up the numbers to multiply. Some of you are looking hard at Marcus's strategy and thinking that he changed the numbers. Marcus, can we come back to your strategy and spend some focused time on it? We can help you think through it more and see whether or not there's something we need to revise.

Ms. Lind ends this warm-up listening to the students' ideas and questions and tells them that in the next few days they will address the questions that arose today. She's out of time to help the class think more about what went wrong in Marcus's strategy, so she assures them she will return to his strategy. This one problem, 25 × 18, generated many different ideas (which was Ms. Lind's goal for the discussion) and, as this short excerpt demonstrates, took the class into a broad mathematical terrain of interrelated concepts, procedures, representations, and explanations. Using the structure of open strategy sharing allowed the class to express and draw upon their ideas but not to linger extensively on any one idea. To spend more time on individual ideas, Ms. Lind needs to plan for targeted discussion.

Targeted Sharing: Two Follow-Ups to Mental Math

The open strategy sharing allows Ms. Lind to size up what ideas she needs to work on further with her students and to plan for a targeted discussion. She makes these decisions in the context of her unit and grade-level goals. For example, her students might benefit from dissecting a compensation strategy (i.e., rounding one of the numbers and adjusting the product, as Marcus attempted to do) or developing their skilled use of arrays to produce a representation about why Faduma or Celia's strategies worked. Ms. Lind wants her students to ground their use and justification of numerical strategies in both array and grouping models. She also wants them to learn to contextualize their strategies in story problems. These are two ideas emphasized in the Common Core State Standards for Mathematical Practice (Common Core 2012). She recognizes that she cannot meet all of her goals in one discussion, and her students could benefit from a focused discussion on using models and creating story problems. These observations lead Ms. Lind to plan for targeted discussions, which bring to the foreground particular concepts, procedures, representations, and explanations.

To illustrate a bit more deeply what we mean by targeted discussion, we offer two brief examples. Ms. Lind could use the targeted discussion structures Why? Let's Justify and Troubleshoot and Revise to highlight important mathematics that emerged from the open strategy sharing discussion. Please note that in the first example, we use an array model for multiplication, and in the second example, we purposefully switch to using a grouping model in order to show the possible choices that Ms. Lind could make. You'll be able to read more about Why? Let's Justify and Troubleshoot and Revise in Chapters 4 and 7.

Example 1: Why? Let's Justify

Connecting numerical strategies to a visual model is one way of making sense of why a strategy works; the model serves as a resource for children to verify their attempts at breaking apart a problem into smaller chunks. The goal of the Why? Let's Justify discussion structure is to figure out why a particular mathematical strategy works. Let's drop in on Ms. Lind's class as she leads a discussion to go further with the class in explaining the steps Faduma took.

Ms. Lind: Yesterday as we were listening to people solve 25 times 18, I realized it has been a while since we worked with arrays. I thought an array would be useful to explain what is happening when we break apart numbers to make a problem easier and how to make sure we've accounted for 18 groups of 25.

Ms. Lind puts an array on the board with Faduma's solution beneath it (see Figure 1.6) and asks students to draw, mark up, and label the array in their journals so that it matches this numerical strategy.

Figure 1.6 Ms. Lind draws an open array to show Faduma's strategy.

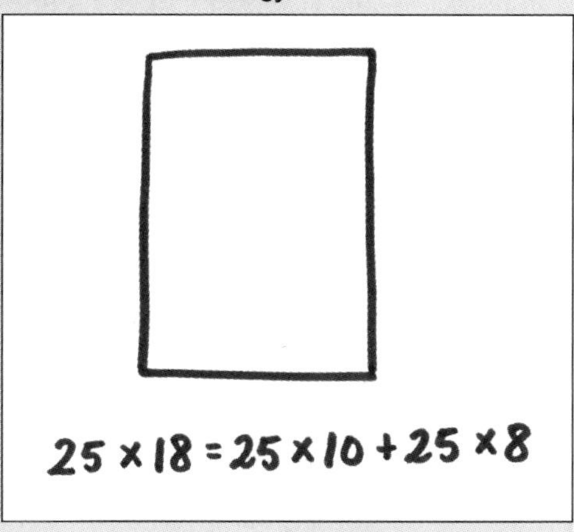

By walking around the room as students are working with the array in their journals, Ms. Lind can make purposeful choices about which students she will invite to share. She lingers over the shoulder of Celeste, who is dividing up the 18 into 10s and 1s, and thinks this idea will provide good fodder for agreement and possibly disagreement about how the array can match Faduma's solution. She is interested in inviting Celeste to share not only for her interesting ideas but also because Celeste tends to be quieter during discussions, and Ms. Lind is working to help her see herself as someone with good ideas. She kneels down next to Celeste and asks her if she'd be willing to share her drawing of the array with her classmates. Celeste nods, and Ms. Lind calls the group back together.

Ms. Lind: Celeste has an idea about the array to offer us. Please look up to the screen at this drawing of the array for 25 times 18. I want you to see if you can make sense of how she divided up the array.

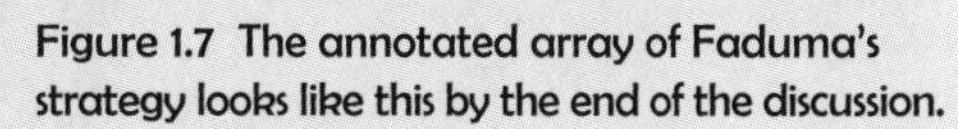

Figure 1.7 The annotated array of Faduma's strategy looks like this by the end of the discussion.

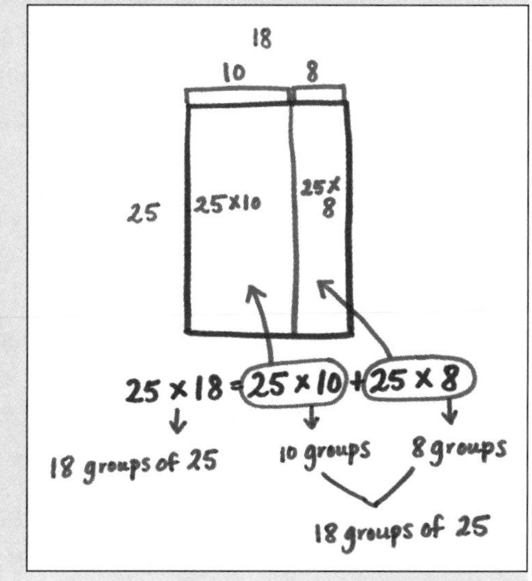

Celeste shares her drawing, explaining how she thought about breaking up the 18 into 10 and 8. As students engage in whole-group and partner sharing about the array, the discussion evolves, with students adding on to prior contributions until a full annotation of the array is shared and it corresponds to the numerical recording of Faduma's strategy (see Figure 1.7).

Ms. Lind's goal is to get to a place where students can see that Faduma's approach began with figuring out 10 groups of 25 and then adding on 8 more groups of 25 to end up with 18 groups of 25 altogether. This targeted sharing asks the class to focus in on one solution and explicitly map the connections between the symbolic and visual representation. In Chapter 4 we dig more deeply into how the teacher navigates these discussions to support student sharing and orient students to one another and the mathematics.

Example 2: Troubleshoot and Revise

It can be quite powerful for a classroom community when students share ideas that aren't quite right yet and seek the help of their classmates. A student seeking peer feedback is valued as having a good kernel of an idea that needs to be developed, and his or her classmates can be motivated to work through the issue. Ms. Lind could use the Troubleshoot and Revise discussion structure to help Marcus and his classmates make sense of where Marcus's strategy went astray and how to revise it to make it work. This lesson could take place the same or next day. After being asked whether he felt comfortable conferring with his classmates to find an answer to his question, Marcus willingly recaps his strategy aloud.

Marcus: I did 20 times 25 to get 500 and then I subtracted 2 to get 498. I kind of think it should work because 20 is just two more than 18. But I'm not sure why I'm not getting the same answer as Faduma. I think I should be.

Ms. Lind could ask students to use an array model to help students troubleshoot and revise Marcus's strategy, and if this discussion actually followed on the heels of the first vignette in this chapter, it would be appropriate for Ms. Lind to use the same model. However, to broaden the representations we use and to provide an example of how contextualizing the numbers and operation in a situation can also be helpful with the revision process, we are going to use a grouping model in this next vignette.

Ms. Lind: Marcus had a great way of beginning this problem. By changing the 18 to 20, he started by making the problem easier for himself. It might help us to put these numbers into a story. Let's imagine Marcus had 25 packs of colored pencils, with 18 pencils in each pack.

As she says this, Ms. Lind values Marcus's idea that he needed to make an adjustment when he rounded one of the factors to 20. Often students are not completely wrong, and we can highlight their good thinking. She is also intentionally selecting a familiar problem context to make sense of the changes to the numbers.

Andre: Oh, I see. When Marcus changed the numbers to 20 times 25, it made it like there were 25 packs of pencils with 20 pencils in each pack. But, we need to have 18 pencils in each pack, not 20!

Ms. Lind: Okay, let's draw the 25 packs of pencils with 20 pencils in each pack.

Drawing these new pencil packs can help the class keep in mind what happened as Marcus's numbers changed from 18 to 20.

Ms. Lind: So, what needs to be removed from each pack to go back to having 18 pencils in a pack instead of 20?

She uses partner talk to engage all the students in considering how to take two pencils out of each pack and how to change the drawing to make it match 25 × 18 (see Figure 1.8). Ms. Lind circulates among the students as

Figure 1.8 These notes on the board supported Marcus in revising his strategy.

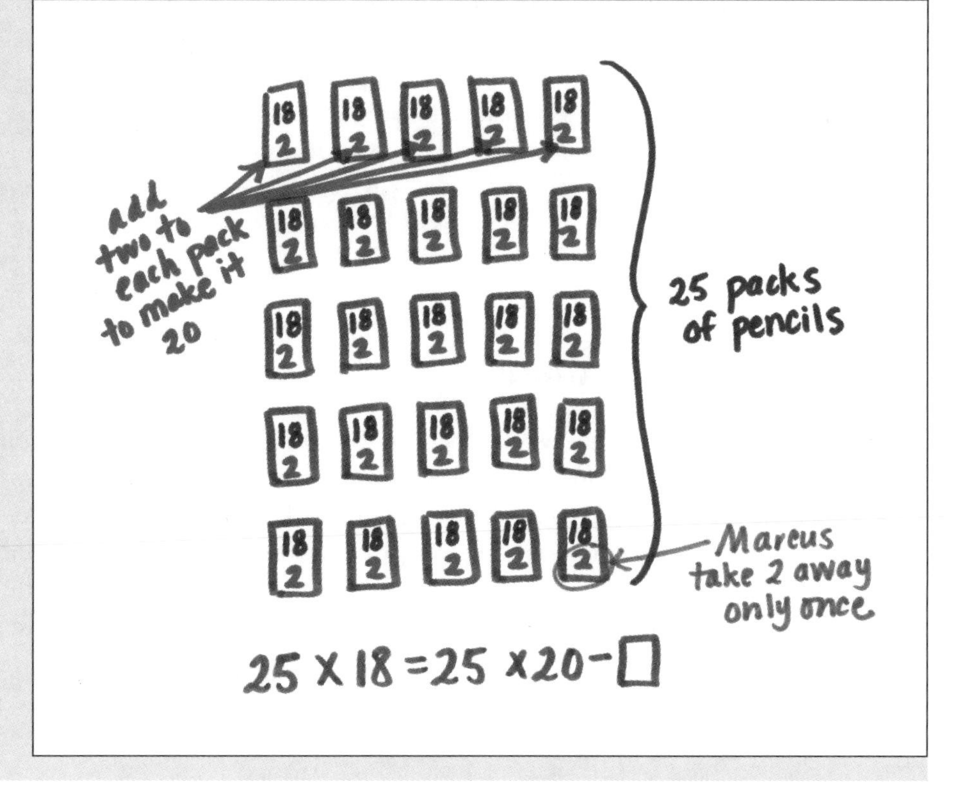

partners discuss this problem to select who should alter the drawing on the board. The drawing can be annotated to show that 50 pencils altogether need to be removed from the product. This will clarify what happened when Marcus subtracted 2 from only 1 of the packs instead of removing 2 from all 25 packs.

Ms. Lind ends the discussion by asking the class to revise Marcus's strategy.

Ms. Lind: Okay, we have worked together to figure out why Marcus's answer was different. Who can say again why his answer was different?

Together the class concludes that when Marcus changed the problem to 25 × 20, he needed to subtract 25 groups of 2 to make sure each pack only had 18 pencils.

Ms. Lind: *(Summarizing the group's thinking as she writes on the board.)* So it looks like we agree that the equation that shows Marcus's strategy should read 25 times 18 is the same as 25 times 20 minus 50.

She hands out an exit card posing a new problem: "How would 15 times 20 need to be adjusted in order to solve 15 times 19?" As a formative assessment strategy, the exit cards help her see how this discussion helped students think about using a compensation strategy. Students fill out these exit cards at the close of a lesson. Ms. Lind will review them in order to assess what students are learning and what they might still be grappling with. What she learns from the exit cards will help her plan for subsequent lessons. You can read more about Troubleshoot and Revise in Chapter 7.

Looking Ahead

We believe that the way teachers and students talk with one another in the classroom is critical to what students learn about mathematics and how they come to see themselves as mathematical thinkers. In our classrooms students should feel that they belong and that they can be successful. Talk is an important way to build that sense of community and to help children grapple with important mathematical ideas. Group discussions can energize children if we are careful about how we teach children to listen to, respond to, and engage with one another's ideas. The time we invest in helping our students learn to participate productively in discussions can result in a huge payoff.

We hope the short vignettes in this chapter begin to help you see our principles at work and the differences between open strategy sharing and targeted discussions. In open strategy sharing, Ms. Lind and her students came up with several ways of thinking about 25 × 18. Targeted discussion helped Ms. Lind zoom in on a few key ideas that came up in the open strategy share. In the rest of this book, we dig more deeply into these structures.

Chapter 2 describes open strategy sharing in more depth. We discuss situations in which teachers might choose an open strategy share and how teachers can lead the discussion to help students listen and contribute to the discussion without getting bored or lost.

We begin our discussion of targeted discussions in Chapter 3 with a structure that naturally extends open strategy sharing, Compare and Connect. The important difference between open strategy sharing and Compare and Connect is that in Compare and Connect the teacher not only elicits strategies but also asks students to find the mathematical similarities and/or differences among them.

We want students to develop a repertoire of strategies, but we also want them to be able to explain why those strategies work. Chapter 4 takes us back to the Why? Let's Justify structure. The goal is to generate justifications for why a mathematical strategy makes sense. This type of discussion typically focuses on just one kind of strategy or procedure. The students are all oriented toward producing a viable explanation. This chapter will help you understand the difference between describing the steps in a strategy and justifying them.

While it is possible to solve some problems in many different ways, students also need opportunities to become more selective about when to use a particular strategy. Chapter 5 takes on this issue by describing a structure we call What's Best and Why? In this discussion structure, the teacher begins not by eliciting ways to solve a particular problem but by (1) showcasing a particular strategy and then asking students to generate an effective use of that strategy or (2) showing a few different ways to solve a problem and asking students to figure out which is the most efficient strategy for this problem.

Teachers often introduce new mathematical models (e.g., number line or array), tools (e.g., a tens frame, the hundreds chart), vocabulary, or notations into mathematical discussions. Models, tools, vocabulary, and notations are all considered mathematical objects. Chapter 6 will highlight how those objects could be the focus of a discussion structure we call Define and Clarify. We consider when such discussions could occur (e.g., when models, tools, terms, and notations are first being introduced or when students have had a chance to use, say, a certain model, but the teacher wants to refine its use). The teacher orchestrates these discussions by modeling the use of the new model, tool, or idea and helps students determine incorrect versus correct usage of that mathematical object.

Chapter 7 more closely deals with how teachers can use errors as opportunities for advancing mathematical thinking through Troubleshoot and Revise, a discussion structure you've already glimpsed. This chapter showcases teachers prompting students to reconcile different strategies in order to defend the correctness of one of the solutions or to engage in a conversation with classmates to find where missteps occurred in a problem-solving attempt and what revisions are needed.

We end the book by summarizing in Chapter 8 the big ideas we've shared and by providing guidance about how to choose goals for discussion and make productive use of the discussion structures within your own curriculum.

To support your teaching, we've included a set of planning templates for the various discussion structures (Appendixes A-F). We've also provided several lesson protocols from the routine instructional activities that appear throughout the book (Appendixes G-I). And, finally, you will also find a list of books and videos available on the web that can help you envision some of the practices and moves you'll see described in the vignettes (Appendix J).

CHAPTER 2

OPEN STRATEGY SHARING

Chances are if you've asked children to share their thinking about a math problem, you've led an open strategy sharing discussion. Open strategy sharing is typically the first way to get mathematical discussions going in classrooms. It's like having a good, basic recipe for a soup from which you can make all kinds of variations. Open strategy sharing allows you to nurture the norms needed for a productive math-talk community. And you can use this discussion structure to model how students should talk with one another.

Too often we associate being good at mathematics with being fast and correct the first time through. We love how Sarah Michaels, Mary Catherine O'Connor, and Megan Williams Hall (2010) describe intelligence:

> *Intelligence is much more than an innate ability to think quickly and stockpile bits of information. Intelligence is a set of problem-solving and reasoning capabilities along with the habits of mind that lead one to use those capabilities regularly. It is also a set of beliefs about one's right and obligation to understand and make sense of the world and one's capacity to figure things out over time. Intelligent habits of mind are learned through daily expectations placed on the learner. By calling on students to use the skills of intelligent thinking—and by holding them responsible for doing so—educators can teach intelligence.* (2)

Over time, as students experience themselves and their classmates as people with good mathematical ideas, you will see a big difference in how much they're willing to persevere and take risks in front of one another.

What Is Open Strategy Sharing?

Many mathematics problems lend themselves to multiple solutions. In open strategy sharing, students listen for and contribute different ways to solve the same problem. The teacher asks *how* questions, such as "How did you think about the problem?" and sometimes *why* questions, like "Why did you start with the seven?" Most important, the teacher invites children to share by asking, "Who did it a different way?" Students are oriented to tracking and repeating their classmates' strategies to show they understand what their peers did. The goal of open strategy sharing is to bring out a range of possible ways to solve the same problem and build students' repertoire of strategies.

How Do You Get Started?

Before you begin open strategy sharing, you'll need to decide on a set of norms for doing mathematics in your classroom and you'll need to think about the "talk moves" you, the teacher, want to use to get discussions underway.

Norms for Doing Mathematics

Teachers introduce and cultivate norms in the classrooms in many different ways. Whatever your method, we think it's important to pay explicit attention to the norms you want to foster. We offer the following list of norms as a way of bringing to life the principles we introduced in Chapter 1. This particular list was inspired by the Standards for Mathematical Practice in the Common Core State Standards (2012), norms suggested by one of our favorite books, *Classroom Discussions* (Chapin, O'Connor, and Anderson 2009), and norms we've seen at play in many classrooms with productive and nurturing learning environments.

In this class, we will do the following:

- Make sense of mathematics

  We think all children should see mathematics as a subject that needs to make sense to them. We don't want children to follow procedures just because their teachers, parents, or peers tell them to.
- Keep trying even when problems are challenging

  Mathematics often has been seen as a school subject that students excel in because they are fast. Not all mathematics problems can be solved in a split second. Problem solving takes planning, strategizing, and persistence.
- Remember that it's okay to make mistakes and revise our thinking

  Children must feel comfortable to take risks, to put out partial ideas or ideas that are still in development, and to stumble when they are learning something new. Being able to revise one's thinking gives students the message that first-draft thinking is welcome in mathematics as much as it is valued in writing instruction.
- Share our mathematical ideas with our classmates (whether we are using words, numbers, pictures, gestures, or tools)

  Words are not the only way to display mathematical ideas. And sometimes informal language, gestures, and diagrams can convey ideas that we cannot yet fully articulate in words. English language learners, students new to an idea, students with special learning needs, and even quiet students can be supported to participate productively by knowing that verbal participation is not the only way to show understanding.
- Listen to understand someone else's idea; give each other time to think

  Listening is as important to learning as is talking and sharing your ideas in other ways. Teaching what to listen for and how to listen is an important part of creating a community of learners that moves one another's ideas forward.
- Ask questions that help us better understand the mathematics

  You'll notice that we care a lot about the messages students receive regarding what it means to be "smart." Asking questions of one another is a way to show that we are listening and trying to understand. Asking questions also shows that we are curious about the mathematics and that we care that children are making sense of the ideas. We want to frame questions as an important part of the learning process and help students to understand that asking a question doesn't mean they are wrong or that we are revealing something that they should have known.

- Agree and disagree with mathematical ideas, not with each other
  Being able to agree and disagree with the mathematics being discussed is an important part of examining or questioning mathematical ideas. But disagreeing with an idea can be socially uncomfortable. Knowing that it is the mathematical idea, not the person, you are disagreeing with can make disagreeing feel safer and productive.
- Remember that everyone has good mathematical ideas
  In a classroom community, all members bring important thinking and ideas to the discussion. Helping students recognize their own and their classmates' thinking and remembering that there is logic within each person's idea is important for a thriving mathematical community. It's important for students to have experiences where they are able to solve problems by putting their minds together to verify ideas. The teacher is not the sole authority of knowledge.

There are many different ways to set up norms in our classrooms, and this list is by no means the only or the best one. But we hope it will inspire you to generate norms that will support your classroom community. Figure 2.1 shows a similar list developed by a school we have worked closely with. It is used across all kindergarten through fifth-grade classrooms. It may be powerful for you to work with your colleagues to nurture a set of expectations that students experience consistently across classrooms in your school or grade level.

Talk Moves

We find the talk moves described by Suzanne Chapin, Catherine O'Connor, and Nancy Anderson (2009) in *Classroom Discussions* enormously useful in helping us think about getting discussions off the ground. The beauty of the authors' five talk moves (see the following table) is that they can guide both teacher talk and student talk. (We've added two additional moves, turn and talk and revise your thinking, to help round out the list.) Many of the teachers with whom we work display and refer to a classroom poster of talk moves that help scaffold student talk (see page 21). See Appendix J for further resources.

Talk Moves to Support Classroom Discussions	
Revoicing *"So you're saying . . ."*	• Repeat some or all of what the student has said, then ask the student to respond and verify whether or not the revoicing is correct. Revoicing can be used to clarify, amplify, or highlight an idea.
Repeating *"Can you repeat what she said in your own words?"*	• Ask a student to repeat or rephrase what another student said. • Restate important parts of complex idea in order to slow the conversation down and dwell on important ideas.
Reasoning *"Do you agree or disagree, and why?"* *"Why does that make sense?"*	• After students have had time to process a classmate's claim, ask students to compare their own reasoning to someone else's reasoning. • Allow students to engage with each other's ideas. • Student: "I respectfully disagree with that idea because . . ."; "This idea makes sense to me because . . ."
Adding On *"Would someone like to add on to this?"*	• Prompt students, inviting them to participate in the conversation or to clarify their own thinking. • Student: "I'd like to add on . . ."
Wait Time *"Take your time . . ."*	• Wait after asking a question before calling on a student. • Wait after a student has been called on to give the student time to organize his or her thoughts. • Student: "I'd like more time . . ."
Turn-and-Talk *"Turn and talk to your neighbor . . ."*	• Circulate and listen to partner talk. Use this information to choose whom to call on. • Allow students to clarify and share ideas. • Allow students to orient themselves to each other's thinking.
Revise *"Has anyone's thinking changed?"* *"Would you like to revise your thinking?"*	• Allow students to revise their thinking as they have new insights. • Student: "I thought . . . But now I think . . . because . . ." "I'd like to revise my thinking."

Figure 2.1 Discussion Expectations

Figure 2.2 Talk Moves

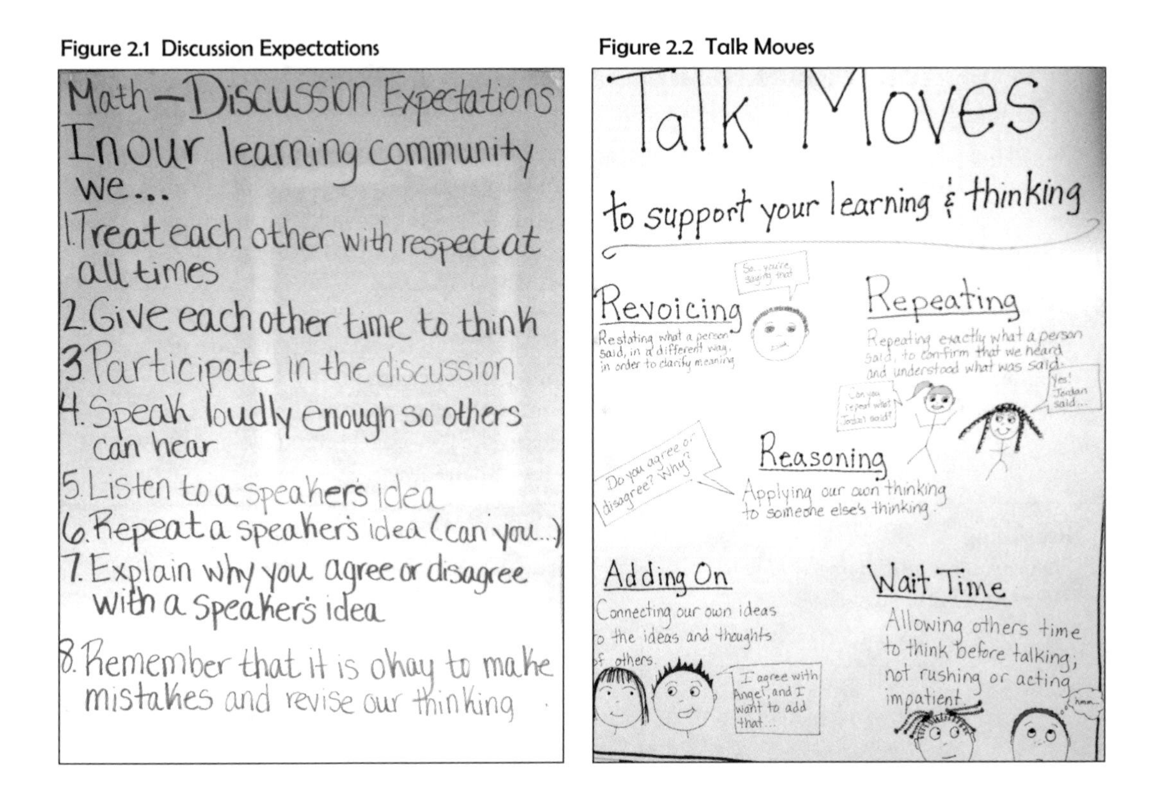

Planning for Open Strategy Sharing in Your Classroom

Getting started planning an open strategy sharing session is rather straightforward. You begin by selecting a problem that has multiple viable solution paths. Listing possible solutions for your own reference can help you anticipate what you might hear from students. You could choose to give students time to solve the problem and share ideas on paper or with a partner to give you advanced notice of your students' strategies. Or you could call on students and learn about their strategies along with your students.

Here's a protocol to help you plan and facilitate the talk (see also the planning template in Appendix A):

- Pick a problem that can be solved in more than one way. Anticipate what children might do to solve the problem.
- Decide whether you want children to work on their own, in partners, or in groups to solve the problem.

- Pose the problem, making sure students understand the problem and have a way to get started. Take anecdotal records while they work.
- Have students share out two to four different ways to solve the problem. Use talk moves (see preceding table and Figure 2.2) and clear representation to help students understand what they hear.
- Close by highlighting the different ways students thought about the problem.

It's important to note that you do not begin an open strategy sharing session by modeling a particular way to solve the problem. Instead, your job is to select a problem that you know students would be able to solve in a number of different ways. Choosing such a task honors the principle that children are sense makers.

Strategy sharing provides a good opportunity to set up norms and practice basic talk and listening moves. Students learn how to talk about their ideas and how to engage with others' ideas, reinforcing the idea that students need support in order to know what and how to share. Students can be supported by what the teacher says or what the teacher attends to. For example, a teacher might say, "Did you all just hear what Elijah said? He said he wanted to 'revise his thinking.' That's what we say in our classroom when you want to change your idea." By saying this, the teacher is supporting students in knowing that revising ideas is something mathematicians do in this classroom and that it's easy to signal a change by saying, "I'd like to revise my thinking." You can also give support by posting sentence stems that help students know how to share mathematical ideas in a discussion (see word bubbles in Figure 2.2).

Open Strategy Sharing In Action

Let's drop in on an intermediate classroom and a primary classroom as they engage in open strategy sharing discussions. The following two vignettes show how two different teachers, Mr. William and Ms. Jenkins, and their students bring out a range of possible ways to solve a problem and build students' repertoire of strategies. The italicized narration provides insight into the teacher's thinking about the decisions he or she is making.

Let's begin by listening in on Mr. William's fourth graders as they have an open strategy sharing discussion about a task called Quick Images. Quick Images as a teaching activity appears in the *Investigations in Number, Data, and Space* curriculum (http://investigations.terc.edu/) but can also be found in a

Figure 2.3 Mr. William's Planning Template for Open Strategy Sharing About Quick Images

Open Strategy Sharing		
Problem to Pose Pose quick image		
Why I Chose This Problem	Applying multiplication strategies to count all; seeing and using groups of dots to count how many	
Opening the Lesson	Brief intro to keep eyes on document camera. "Today, we are working on sharing different ways of figuring out how many dots."	
How might my students solve this problem?	**Who solved it this way?**	**Who should share today?**
3 groups of 6 and then 3 more	Mark	Just share out—look for students who have not shared recently
3 groups of 7 dots		
3 fours and 3 threes		
Notes to Myself About What I'm Looking for How are students decomposing the image to keep track of how many?		
Other Strategies That Emerged During the Lesson		
6 groups of 3 and 3 ones	Neeyah	
Closing the Lesson	Reinforce that there are different ways to decompose and see the image.	

range of other elementary curricula. The teacher shows an arrangement of dots or objects for three seconds, asking students to create a mental representation of the quantity in order to figure out how many objects they saw. This activity builds children's ability to compose and decompose a quantity in a variety of ways (see Shumway [2011] and Storeygard [2009] for examples of Quick Images in action). The brevity in viewing encourages subitizing.

Open Strategy Sharing Through Quick Images in a Fourth-Grade Classroom

As his fourth-grade students prepare to participate in the familiar classroom routine of Quick Images, Mr. William uses a document camera to display the image he has selected to reinforce thinking about multiplication as finding the total of equal groups of objects. Mr. William plans to use this Quick Image activity to elicit three to five different strategies for finding the total. (Figure 2.3 shows Mr. William's planning notes.) Students squirm a bit in their desks, although their eyes steadily gaze toward the task displayed by the document camera, in eager anticipation of the activity.

Mr. William: Three seconds! I'm going to show you an image of dots for only three seconds, and your job is to figure out how many dots you see. I want you to pay attention to how you see the dots so you can share your strategy with us. Remember, you get to see each image twice.

Using the document camera, Mr. William flashes an image of three groups of seven dots (Figure 2.4).

He flashes the image for three seconds. After the first flash, he invites students to think independently.

Figure 2.4 **Mr. William displays this Quick Image first for the open strategy sharing session.**

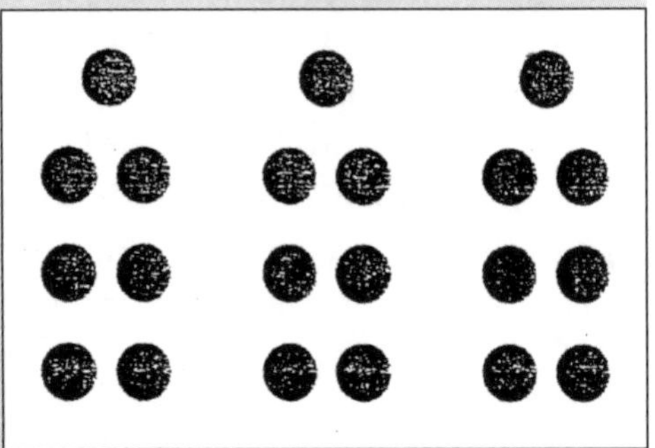

Mr. William: What did you see? How did you see it?

Modeling quiet think time, Mr. William closes his eyes and then speaks using a whisper.

Mr. William: Hold on to that. Here it comes again. Check what you think you saw. Maybe you want to revise your answer. *(After the second flash.)* Would it help you if you drew what you saw? Go ahead and sketch on your whiteboard if that feels helpful to you.

Students begin sketching the image on their individual whiteboards, and some whisper to their neighboring classmates about what they saw. Mr. William observes their work.

Mr. William: How many did you get? Let me hear your answers. Shout it out!

Mr. William has chosen to invite students to shout out their answers because this first problem was very accessible to all students. As he looked at the sketches on their whiteboards and listened to their whispers, he could see and hear that three groups of seven was an easy entry point for the students.

Class: *(In unison.)* 21!
Mr. William: Does anyone have a different answer?

There are no responses. Mr. William asks this question even when he is not expecting to hear a different answer. If teachers don't ask it, they are reinforcing quick correct answers again, and students don't have opportunities to learn from mistakes. If he had heard different numbers among the voices, he would have acknowledged that and said, "I am hearing a couple different numbers, which is just fine. As we work through this, I'll want us to figure out together which one is accurate and why. We often have to revise our thinking in mathematics."

Mr. William: Okay, I'm going to ask you to share different ways you saw the dots. Mark, what did you see?
Mark: *(Speaking softly.)* It's a pattern. I can see 7 three times, or 7 plus 7 plus 7, and that's 21.
Mr. William: Mark, I want you to say that again and speak loudly so everyone can hear your idea. *(Turning to the whole class.)* Our job as listeners is to follow what Mark is saying.

As Mr. William asks Mark to speak loudly he is supporting students in knowing how to share so their ideas are understandable to others. As he reminds students of their job as listeners he is also supporting students in knowing how to listen.

Mr. William: *(After Mark repeats his strategy.)* So you saw 7 dots in a group. How did you see the 7 dots?
Mark: I saw a chunk of 6 and then 1 above it. *(He moves his finger in the air as if he is showing the 6 and 1.)*
Mr. William: *(Circling the dots on the image under the document camera as Mark has described. [See Figure 2.5.])* Okay, so you saw 6 and 1, which makes 7, and you saw that group of 7 three times. We see just what you did. This is one good way. Who saw the dots in a different way? Neeyah?

Neeyah: Kind of like Mark—I saw that the same group happened 3 times. But I wasn't sure how many were in each group. So I counted 3 and 3 and then the 1.

Mr. William: Can you come up and point to show us where you saw the 3 and 3 and 1?

Neeyah: *(Pointing to the dots and circling them with her finger.)* Here they are!

Mr. William: Ah, yes. *(Turning to the class as he recircles Neeyah's groups. [See Figure 2.6.])* Here is the 3 and 3 and 1 that Neeyah saw. And, Neeyah, how did you know how many there were all together?

Neeyah: I counted all the threes, like 3, 6, 9, 12, 15, 18, and then I counted the ones: 19, 20, 21.

Mr. William: Interesting. You counted by threes and then you counted on by ones. So you saw the dots quickly in 6 groups of 3. Okay, let's find out one more way.

Mr. William continues by inviting one more student to share and then wraps up the discussion by repeating the three different ways students saw the 21 dots and by emphasizing grouping as a foundational idea for multiplication.

Figure 2.5 Mr. William marks up the Quick Image to show how Mark decomposed it.

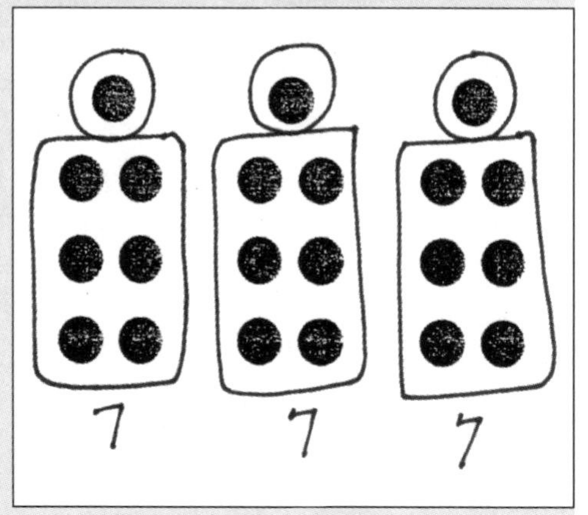

Figure 2.6 Mr. William marks up the Quick Image to show how Neeyah counted all the dots.

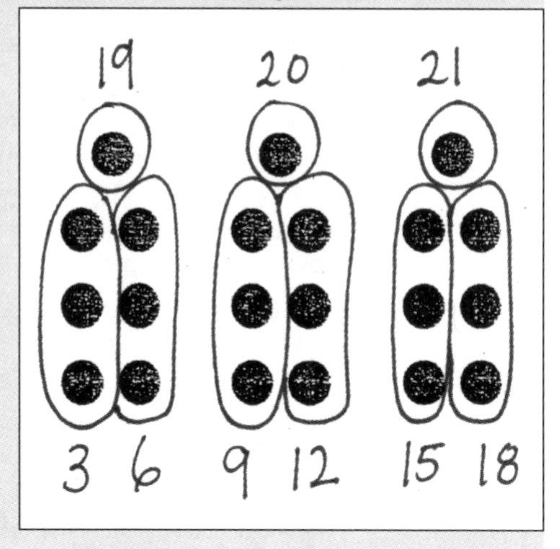

Mr. William supports students in several ways. When he calls on Mark and Neeyah, he follows up on their initial responses by asking them to clarify and show the class how they counted. He uses talk moves to support them to share and clarify what they did for the rest of the class. This is one way of getting discussion going in classrooms; it is clearly directed by the teacher and generally goes back and forth between the teacher and one student at a time. This type of back-and-forth exchange can begin to show students what it means to share their thinking. But it's also possible for some students to check out easily or lose track of what is being discussed. As we visit on a different day in Mr. William's classroom and offer another glimpse into a classroom discussion, notice how he uses talk moves to open up participation more broadly across all the students. His planning notes appear in Figure 2.7.

Figure 2.7 Mr. William's Planning Template for Second Open Strategy Sharing

Open Strategy Sharing		
Problem to pose Pose quick image		
Why I chose this problem	Applying multiplication strategies to count all; seeing and using groups of dots to count how many	
Opening the lesson	Brief intro to keep eyes on document camera. "Your job is to figure out how many dots. I want to hear how you know."	
How might my students solve this problem?	**Who solved it this way?**	**Who should share today?**
9 fours if all were filled out—imagine the group of 4 missing in the middle. $9 \times 4 - 4$	Ayoub	Share second
Fours in columns: 3 fours and then 2 and then 3 more $12 + 8 + 12$	Divina	Start with this one
Counting fours around the perimeter	Olivia	Share third
Notes to myself about what I'm looking for How are students using groups to figure out how many? I really want students to make sense of each other's ideas.		
Other strategies that emerged during the lesson		
Closing the lesson	Reinforce that there are different ways to decompose and see the image.	

Open Strategy Sharing Through Quick Images in a Fourth-Grade Classroom: A Second Session

In this discussion, Mr. William makes intentional moves to broaden who participates and how. He knows his students can share their thinking, but he wants to engage them as listeners to make sense of each other's ideas.

Mr. William: Okay, here comes the image. Remember, your job is to figure out how many dots you see and remember how you saw them. Ready?

He displays the image (Figure 2.8) with the document camera for three seconds, hides it for a few seconds, and then reveals it for another three seconds.

Figure 2.8 Mr. William uses this as the second Quick Image for an open strategy sharing session.

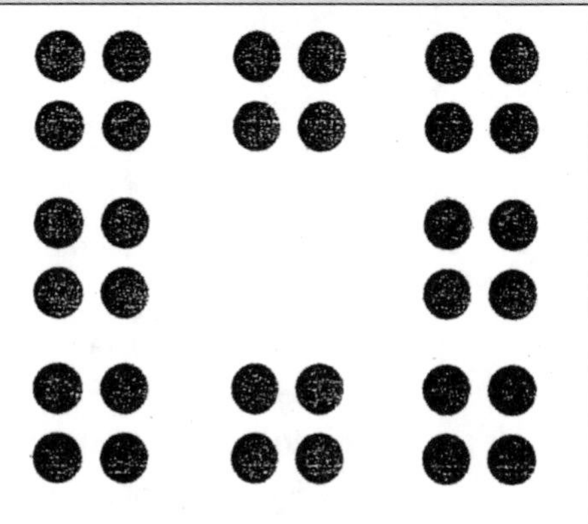

Mr. William: I want you to turn to your neighbor and share how many dots you saw and how you saw the dots. Make sure you both share. See if you have the same way or a different way.

By inviting the children to do a turn-and-talk about their solutions, Mr. William provides an opportunity for every student to share their strategy. He also has an opportunity to walk around the room and listen in to hear a range of ideas and to think about which ideas he wants to elicit.

Mr. William: I can hear a lot of interesting thinking. Let's come back together and share your solutions. I want to start with Divina. Divina, how did you think about this image? As you explain, I'll try to record what you saw.

Divina: *(Walking up to the screen and using her finger to point.)* I saw little groups of 4, and I saw 3 groups of 4 here *(pointing to the left-hand column)* and then 2 groups of 4 *(pointing to the middle column)* and then 3 more groups of 4 *(pointing to the right-hand column)*.

Mr. William: Okay, let's stop there for a moment to make sure we all understand how you saw the groups of 4. Can someone repeat how Divina saw the groups of 4? Jose?

Mr. William will ask students to repeat their classmates' thinking at strategic and useful moments throughout the discussion. Repeating another person's idea helps students pay attention to each other's strategies to show they understand what their peers did. Putting their classmates' strategies in their own words allows students to practice and develop their academic language.

Jose: She said she saw them, like, in *(gesturing his hand up and down)* . . . um . . .

Mr. William: Columns? Are you showing columns with your hand? *(Jose nods.)* A column is a section that goes up and down. Okay, go on, Jose.

By the hand gestures Jose was using, Mr. William could see that he understood Divina's strategy for seeing the groups of four in columns. For Jose, an English language learner, and for many students, hand gestures are an important part of conveying what they mean. In this instance, Mr. William gave the student the mathematical word to use and supported him in showing his understanding.

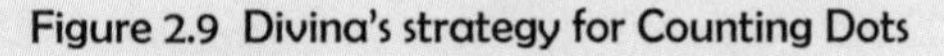
Figure 2.9 Divina's strategy for Counting Dots

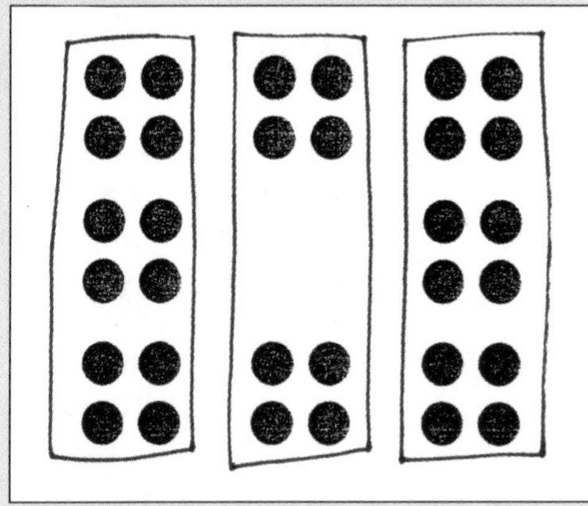

Jose: And she saw them like a column of 3, then a column of 2, and then 1 more column of 3 groups. (See Figure 2.9.)

Mr. William: Thank you, Jose. Divina, is that how you saw the dots? *(Divina nods, and Mr. William turns to the class.)* Do you think you could repeat to your neighbor what Jose just said about how Divina saw the dots in columns? *(Students turn and talk.)*

Mr. William now uses a turn-and-talk for a slightly different purpose. He wants to make sure everyone is on board with the strategy before moving on to a new one. It is another way his students are oriented to tracking and repeating others' strategies to show they understand what their peers did.

Mr. William: Let's come back together. Divina, how many dots did you see all together?

Divina: Thirty-two.

Mr. William: Who saw the dots the same way as Divina? *(Some students raise their hands.)* Who saw the dots in a different way? Ayoub?

Ayoub: I did. I saw groups of 4 also, but when I had to figure out how many groups there were, I filled in that hole in the middle. (See Figure 2.10.)

Mr. William: What hole?

Ayoub: *(Pointing to the middle.)* Right there. Like, if there were 3 columns with 3 groups of 4 in each column.

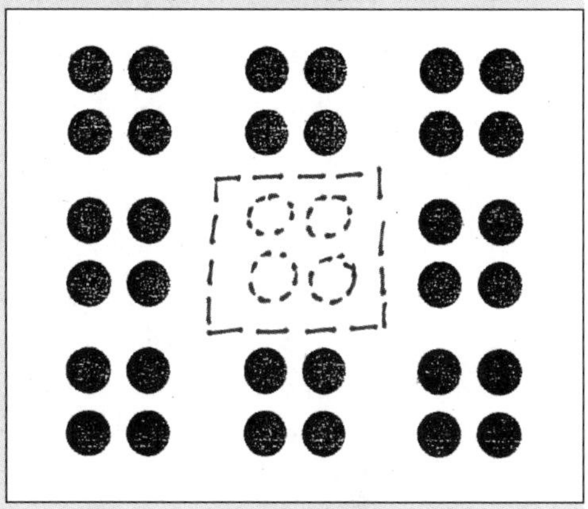

Mr. William: *(To the class.)* Do you see the hole Ayoub is talking about? *(Students nod.)* Okay, go on.

Ayoub: So I knew if there were 9 groups of 4, that would be 36. But I had to take away that group of 4 in the middle that I had added.

Figure 2.10 Ayoub's Strategy for Counting Dots

Mr. William: How did you do that?

Ayoub: I went 36, 35, 34, 33.

Mr. William: Okay. I hear you counting back to remove the 4. Can you use the number line to show us how you took those 4 away?

Ayoub: *(Pointing to 36 on the number line on the classroom wall and making jumps with his finger in the air.)* I start here and I jump back 1, 2, 3, 4. Wait, that's 32. I have to jump 4 times, so that's 32 I guess. I'm not sure why. I kind of think it should be 33.

Mr. William: Do you have another way to help you examine why that strategy isn't working?

Ayoub: Yeah, right, so if I didn't use the number line, I might just think 35, 34, 33, 32. Yeah, I see I should say the 36, but then count back from there. Yeah, I get it, it's 32. It's 32.

Mr. William: Okay, Ayoub, we hear the way you are revising your answer. You seem to be convinced now that your answer is 32. I want to be sure we're following what Ayoub said. It's important that you know you can ask Ayoub a question if you'd like to hear more about his choices. We may not always do a turn-and-talk, but you can jump in and ask.

Knowing Ayoub had made an error in his counting back, Mr. William is mindful of how to support him through this common misstep and position him as competent at the same time. Because Mr. William asks Ayoub if he has a different way, Ayoub finds a resolution to his error. Treating errors as important learning opportunities and a natural part of mathematical thinking maintains the norm that errors, even in intermediate grades, are not shameful. Mr. William is also shaping discussion expectations in his class by empowering students to be intent listeners and ask questions when they are not sure what a classmate did.

Savell: So, Ayoub said that he realized there were only 8 groups because if you count the three groups of 4 by threes, you'd have 9 groups of 4?

Ayoub: Yeah, I could see it sort of looked like a tic-tac-toe game, and there's 3 groups, 3 groups, and 3 groups.

Mr. William: I really liked that you asked Ayoub to say more about his thinking. Let me see who used the same strategy as Ayoub. *(Five students raise their hand.)* Ayoub, you can see who was thinking like you on this problem. Well, we don't see everyone's hands, and we have time to hear one more way. Who has a different way than Divina and Ayoub? Olivia?

Olivia: I saw 8 groups of 4. And 8 times 4 is 32.

Mr. William: You saw 8 groups of 4. How many other people saw 8 groups of 4? Olivia, how did you know there were 8 groups?

Olivia: I started up here *(pointing to the upper left-hand group of dots)* and then I just continued around counting all the groups *(pointing in a clockwise circle around)*. (See Figure 2.11.)

Figure 2.11 Olivia's Strategy for Counting Dots

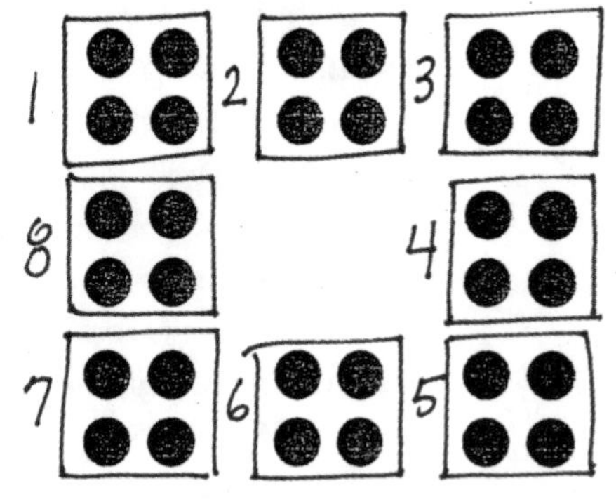

Mr. William: Let's see if we understand what Olivia did. Who can repeat what Olivia said? Hapsa?

Hapsa: She just went around. Like, 1, 2, 3, 4, 5, 6, 7, 8. Eight groups.

Mr. William: Is that right, Olivia? *(Olivia nods.)* Okay, and how did you know that 8 groups of 4 is 32?

Olivia: I just know it. That's a fact for me.

Mr. William: You just know that one. Okay. *(Turning to the class.)* Do you agree with Olivia that 8 groups of 4, or 8 times 4 is 32? *(Students nod.)* Can we write a number sentence for what Olivia did? What would that look like? Emran?

Emran: It would be 8 times 4 equals 32. *(Mr. William records 8 × 4 = 32 on Olivia's image.)*

Mr. William: Nice. I want you to notice that we figured out three different ways to count out how many dots there were today.

In this discussion, Mr. William makes strategic use of turn-and-talks and the repeating talk move in order to broaden student participation in the discussion. Being mindful of using the talk moves in this way can keep students engaged in the conversation and build the class's ideas together.

Open Strategy Sharing Through Problem Solving in a First-Grade Classroom

Open strategy sharing is not just for older students. Let's take a look at strategy sharing in a first-grade class. Ms. Jenkins routinely creates math problems from the situations that her students experience in the class. Her planning notes appear in Figure 2.12. Familiar problem situations are a nice way for her to build norms for math talk in this classroom and get a sense of the strategies that already make sense to her students.

Ms. Jenkins gathers her class on the rug. Each child has a clipboard. Several baskets of materials such as cubes, hundreds charts, and number lines are within arm's reach of all children. Ms. Jenkins begins by telling the students that she needs some markers for an art project that afternoon. She reads the problem to the class, which says that she has opened a few new packages of markers and wants to fill 4 jars with 5 markers each. How many markers does she need?

Ms. Jenkins: Can you figure out how many markers I'll need?

Students: *(All talking at once.)* Wait, how many? Five?

Ms. Jenkins: Let me read the problem one more time. This time, think about what you're picturing in your mind as I describe this story problem.

Ms. Jenkins's choice to read the whole problem again is an important one. It can be tempting to focus children on just the numbers in a problem or key words that might give them a clue about what operation to use. But, if we want students to be good problem solvers, we need them to make sense of the whole problem situation.

Ms. Jenkins: *(After reading the whole problem again.)* Now, Furgan, tell me what you picture.

Furgan: I saw you standing over there at the art station with 4 jars and putting 5 new fresh markers in them.

Ms. Jenkins: Maybe Furgan's image can help you. Think about me standing there and putting markers into jars.

Figure 2.12 Ms. Jenkins's Planning Template for Open Strategy Sharing

Open Strategy Sharing		
Problem to pose I had 4 jars of markers. I put 5 markers in each jar. How many markers did I have in all?		
Why I chose this problem	• Want students to visualize the problem situation • Want students to be able to model problem with counters, drawings, or an expression	
Opening the lesson	Describe getting ready for an art project	
How might my students solve this problem?	**Who solved it this way?**	**Who should share today?**
Draw a picture with 4 jars and 5 markers in each, with tallies	James	Yes, second
Draw a picture with 4 jars and the number 5 in each	Saraya	Yes, third
Use counters to show each of the jars		
Skip-count by fives	Teresa	Yes, start here
Notes to myself about what I'm looking for Can students show me how their strategy fits the situation? **Watch out for students who combine 5 and 4. Ask them to retell the situation to me. Are they holding on to the whole problem?		
Other strategies that emerged during the lesson		
Closing the lesson	Highlight how the drawing, objects, or number sentence mapped back to the problem. There were different ways our students showed what was happening in the problem.	

Ms. Jenkins pulls out one of the jars and some markers and starts to mime distributing the markers. She's careful not to give too much away because she wants the students to figure out the problem.

Ms. Jenkins: You can get started on the problem. It's okay to ask a neighbor if you have a question.

Students start to draw pictures. Some count on their fingers; others pull out a number line. Still others grab handfuls of cubes. After several minutes of children working quietly, some stopping to look at their neighbors' work, Ms. Jenkins brings them back together.

Ms. Jenkins: Teresa, tell us what you did.
Teresa: I counted all the markers, and my answer is 20.
Ms. Jenkins: What do you mean? Twenty what?
Teresa: Twenty markers. That's how many you'll need.
Ms. Jenkins: Tell us how you counted.
Teresa: Well, I just counted by fives: 5, 10, 15, 20. (See Figure 2.13.)
Ms. Jenkins: Thanks. I hear you saying that you skip-counted by 5 four times.

Figure 2.13 The board shows Teresa's solution.

Ms. Jenkins: How many other people solved it the way Teresa did?

Ms. Jenkins writes down the names of 5 other students who raise their hand.

From this exchange Ms. Jenkins learns more about how one student solved the problem. Ms. Jenkins and the class hear that Teresa knows what the twenty means and that she skip-counted to figure out how many markers were needed. She thought about five markers in each jar.

Using Open Strategy Sharing to Build Norms for Math Talk in a First-Grade Classroom

The rest of the strategy sharing could proceed with Ms. Jenkins asking other students to share their thinking until a range of strategies are documented on the board. By writing down children's names, Ms. Jenkins would have a good sense of which students used which strategies.

As Mr. William did, Ms. Jenkins could also slow down the conversation with each sharer to bring her listeners into the discussion and help students know how to be engaged in a discussion. Doing so would also give Ms. Jenkins valuable information about which mathematical ideas are making sense, which need clarification, and how her students are able to communicate their thinking. The first exchange with Teresa shows Ms. Jenkins asking follow-up questions until important details about Teresa's strategy are made public and available to the class. We'll show next how the conversation could continue to build those norms more explicitly.

Ms. Jenkins: Who solved the problem a different way?

James: I used tally marks.

Ms. Jenkins: Before James tells us what he did with the tally marks, remember that your job as listeners is to see if you can understand what James did. Go ahead, James, describe how the tally marks helped you solve the problem.

James: Well, first I made a jar. Then I put in 5 tally marks.

Ms. Jenkins: I think it would help us to see your picture. Hold it up.

James: I put 5 tally marks in each jar and I counted all my tallies and I made 20. (See Figure 2.14.)

Ms. Jenkins: Let's see if we really understand James's strategy. Sometimes, repeating it is a good way to know. James, you can call on one of your classmates to see if they understand.

Figure 2.14 The board shows James's solution.

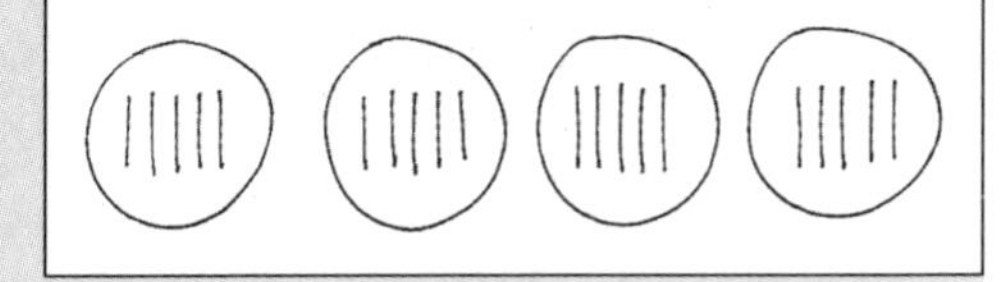

James: Lucy

James passes his journal to Lucy, who stands up and holds it.

Lucy: So, what I think he did was draw circles that showed the jars Ms. Jenkins used. And then each tally mark inside is one marker. And Ms. Jenkins said to put in 5 markers.

Ms. Jenkins: What do you think, James, about what Lucy said?

James: Yeah, that's what I did.

Ms. Jenkins: Now, let me ask you this. Check with your partner to see if you both understand what James's picture shows. What words or labels would you add to the picture to show what the picture means?

Students talk in pairs, pointing up at the picture to show what the picture means. While they do this Ms. Jenkins quickly reproduces the picture on the easel next to her so that all students can see it easily, and she listens to what she hears from the pairs. She makes this turn-and-talk move to bring in all the participants. Asking them to state how they would label the picture is another way that she is working on orienting them to one another's ideas.

Coming up and pointing to the picture is another way to use the diagram and gestures to develop the academic language needed to explain one's strategies.

Ms. Jenkins: Angela and Abdi, why don't you two both come up. I heard you talk about some ways to label this picture.

Ms. Jenkins overheard Angela and Abdi talk about how to label, so she is confident they will contribute to the group. She also knows that Abdi is an English language learner, and she is always mindful of encouraging her students to share their ideas and have a voice in discussions.

Abdi: We say to put "jars" here.
Ms. Jenkins: Go ahead and write that for us.
Abdi: And then we say "5 markers."
Angela: Yeah, you could just label one of the jars with "5 markers" or you could label all of them.
Ms. Jenkins: What do you think, class, of what Angela and Abdi did? Give me a thumbs-up if this makes sense to you or a thumbs-sideways if you're not sure.

Ms. Jenkins sees that her class is indicating with their thumbs that they understand their classmates' suggestions and moves on to another strategy.

Ms. Jenkins makes strategic choices here; she has high expectations for her students and teaches them how to interact, talk, and listen to one another. She thinks carefully about who needs extra support and how students can display their good ideas. The use of students' own work and a public chart allows students to use words, gestures, and drawing to convey how they are thinking.

Summary and Reflection Questions: When Do I Want to Have an Open Strategy Sharing Discussion?

Open strategy sharing provides a strong foundation for mathematics discussions. It helps teachers build wide participation by showing that problems can be solved in different ways. It's important to choose a task that students can make sense of in multiple ways, and by facilitating the conversation you can meet the mathematical goal of recognizing multiple valid strategies. Quick Images and word problems lend themselves to multiple strategies. Charting multiple strategies also helps students begin to build a repertoire of strategies. For example, in the Quick Image example, students counted 36 by skip-counting by 4s, seeing 8 groups of 4, or seeing 9 groups of 4, less 1 group. In the word problem, children were exposed to skip-counting by fives or thinking about four groups of five. Having these initial ideas on the table can begin articulation of generalizable strategies and produce the fodder for more targeted discussions, like the ones that you'll be introduced to in the following chapters.

Socially, open strategy sharing can help you build the norms and discussion expectations that bring to life the principles for productive mathematical talk that are at the center of this book. Children experience themselves and their classmates as competent. They see that their teachers are interested in their ideas, and with the intentional use of talk moves, they learn what it means to listen and make sense of each other's ideas and to revise their thinking.

Before you move on to the next chapter, take a moment to reflect on these questions.

1. What norms do I want to foster in my classroom? Which talk moves do I want to start using in my classroom? How can I make displays that will help my students and me engage in math discussions?
2. In next week's lessons, where do I see opportunities for open strategy sharing?
3. What challenges have I encountered when I have tried to support my students to share their mathematical thinking? How could I use the talk moves or the classroom discussion expectations to overcome these challenges?

CHAPTER 3

TARGETED DISCUSSION: COMPARE AND CONNECT

Now we're rolling! After asking students, "Who solved the problem a different way?" a logical next step is to ask them what makes their strategy the same or different. The discussion structure that we focus on in this chapter, Compare and Connect, helps fine-tune this important kind of classroom conversation.

Planning for a Compare and Connect Discussion in Your Classroom

When you are planning a Compare and Connect discussion, it's important to think carefully about your instructional goal. What mathematical connections do you want your students to make between strategies? It may be helpful to begin by focusing students on comparing two strategies. What makes them similar and/or different mathematically? Make sure you are clear about why it's important for students to notice those similarities and/or differences; they need to know the mathematical value of doing so. As in any discussion, the students should listen to and contribute ideas in order to move toward shared understanding.

You can use the template found in Appendix B to think through the following instructional decisions:

- Decide which strategies you want your students to compare and connect.
- Identify connections that you believe are important for students to notice between the two or more strategies.
- On your planning sheet, write out the strategies like you imagine they will be recorded on the board. (Add more columns to the planning sheet if you are comparing more than two strategies.)
- Anticipate what students may notice as they compare and connect the strategies and how you might respond to support their ideas.
- Jot a note to yourself about the mathematical idea you want to target during the discussion and highlight at the end of the discussion. Put the note in your pocket so you can quickly remind yourself during the discussion.

As you facilitate the discussion, stay focused on the targeted strategies and the key mathematical idea. It can be tempting to pursue other interesting ideas that may emerge (as we do in an open strategy share); however, a Compare and Connect discussion is all about delving into the connections between the strategies of focus. As you will see in the upcoming vignette, Mr. Delgado keeps two particular strategies (counting on by ones and counting on by bigger increments) at the heart of the discussion as he works toward his goal of supporting students in thinking about making tens to make adding more efficient.

First Graders Compare and Connect Two Strategies for Adding

Let's drop in on a Compare and Connect discussion in Mr. Delgado's classroom. After listening to his first graders share their ideas about $7 + 5$ in an open strategy sharing session, Mr. Delgado stands back that afternoon to think about their ideas. Reviewing the chart he made during their open strategy share, he can see students added the two numbers in a range of ways, including counting all by ones, counting on by ones using fingers or a number line, and decomposing five or seven into quantities that allowed students to make ten (see Figure 3.1).

He decides to design a follow-up Compare and Connect discussion focusing on counting on by ones and counting on by bigger increments to make ten; he wants to highlight the idea that decomposing the second quantity into

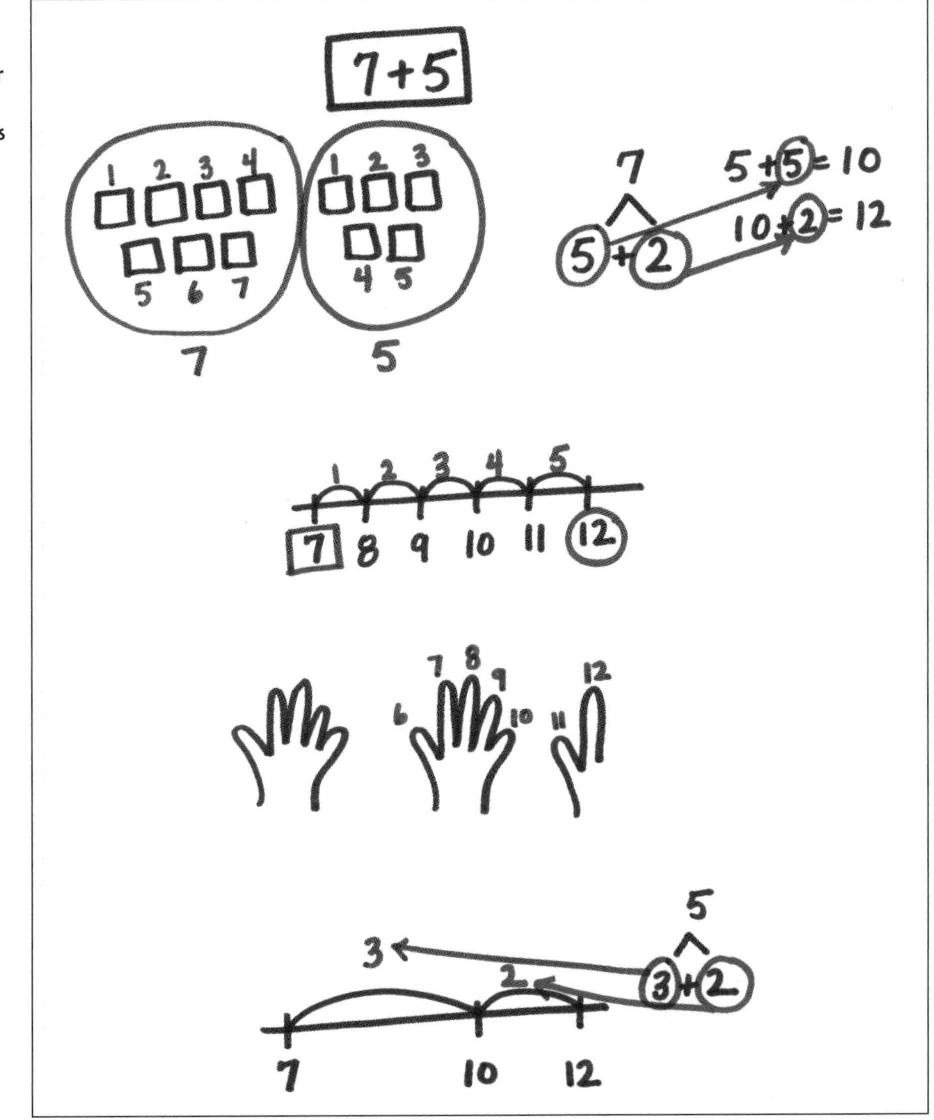

Figure 3.1 Students' strategies for 7 + 5 are noted on this classroom chart.

chunks to make ten is a good strategy for students to use as they work on advancing their strategies. He sits down to quickly sketch out his plan for the next day's discussion. As he prepares, he targets particular solutions to help students think about how you can make decisions about making bigger jumps.

Mr. Delgado is using a previous class discussion as fodder for the Compare and Connect discussion (see Figure 3.2 for his planning notes); this helps us see

Figure 3.2 Mr. Delgado's Planning Template for a Compare and Connect Discussion: Counting On Strategies

Compare and Connect

Strategy 1	Strategy 2
7 + 5 Counting on by ones on fingers or a number line 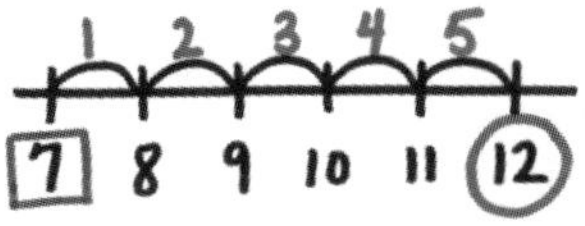 1 2 3 4 5 7 8 9 10 11 12	7 + 5 = 7 + 3 + 2 Split up the 5 into 3 and 2 and combine 7 with 3 to make 10, and then add 2 7 + 5 3 + 2 7 + 3 = 10 10 + 2 = 12

What connections are important for students to notice?

You can start with 7 and count on the five one by one. Or we can break up the five into chunks that allow us to easily make tens.

Supporting students' thinking

What students might notice	How I might respond to support their thinking
Both started at 7.	Why does starting at 7 make sense? How did the strategies use the second number?
Both got 12.	How did the strategy help get to 12?
One broke up 5 and added three numbers: 7, 3, and 2.	Where did the 3 and the 2 come from? Could you break up the 5 into a 4 and a 1? Why was it useful to break the 5 up that way?

What is the key mathematical idea I want to highlight?

Breaking up the second number into chunks that easily make tens makes counting the total efficient.

how open strategy sharing can lead to targeted strategy sharing. Throughout this book, for each of our targeted discussion structures, we offer a planning template that can help you anticipate and think through key ideas that will help you orchestrate the discussions. Your own experiences and lesson planning strategies will help you adapt these, but in our templates we've included the most important ideas that you will need to have ready before you begin each kind of discussion.

Mr. Delgado: Yesterday we were talking about how you might add 7 plus 5, and there were many different ways we thought about this problem.

Referring to the chart from the previous day's discussion, Mr. Delgado briefly recaps each strategy. In doing this he is orienting students to each other and the mathematics. He looks to the students who shared the solutions in order to thank them for their contribution and to ensure he has captured their ideas accurately. He looks to the other students to make sure they understand the solutions so they can delve further during today's discussion.

Mr. Delgado: There is a lot we can learn from thinking more about each of these strategies. Today, I would like us to focus on two particular solutions. Keisha, you solved this problem by counting on by ones. *(Pointing to her solution on the chart.)* Can you model this for us again? *(Looking to the other students.)* Your job right now is to listen to Keisha explain her idea and make sure you understand her thinking.

Mr. Delgado starts by inviting Keisha to share her strategy because he is working toward the mathematical goal of counting on by numbers larger than one. By starting with an example of counting on by ones he hopes to come to a collective understanding of this strategy, name the strategy as "counting on by ones," and use it as a launching point to move to counting on in larger jumps.

Keisha: *(Carrying her number line to the front of the room.)* First I pulled out my number line.

Mr. Delgado: Can we watch you do that and listen to how you counted using the number line?

Keisha: Okay. *(Putting her finger at 7.)* 1, 2, 3, 4, 5.

Mr. Delgado: Go on, what did you do next?

As Mr. Delgado asks Keisha questions such as "Can we watch you do that and listen to how you counted?" and "What did you do next?" he is supporting Keisha and her classmates in knowing what and how to share.

Keisha: Then I saw that I landed on 12. So my answer is 12.

Mr. Delgado: Thank you, Keisha, we see just how you counted. And let me draw a picture of the number line to show what you did (see Figure 3.3). How many other people are comfortable using Keisha's strategy? *(Many hands go up.)* Yes, this strategy makes good sense. You started at 7 on the number line and then you counted on 5 more and landed on 12. Xavier, you thought about the problem a little bit differently. I'd like you to tell us again how you thought about 7 plus 5.

Since Mr. Delgado is working toward the mathematical goal of counting on by larger numbers, he chooses to repeat Keisha's strategy himself (rather than have a student repeat her idea) and moves on to sharing a strategy for counting on by a larger number. He wants the bulk of the discussion to center on the relationship between the two strategies.

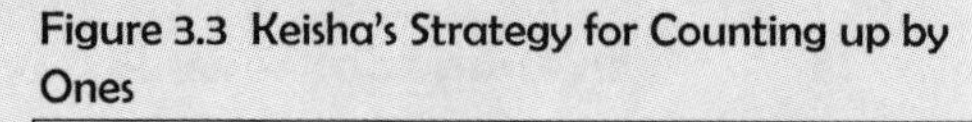

Figure 3.3 Keisha's Strategy for Counting up by Ones

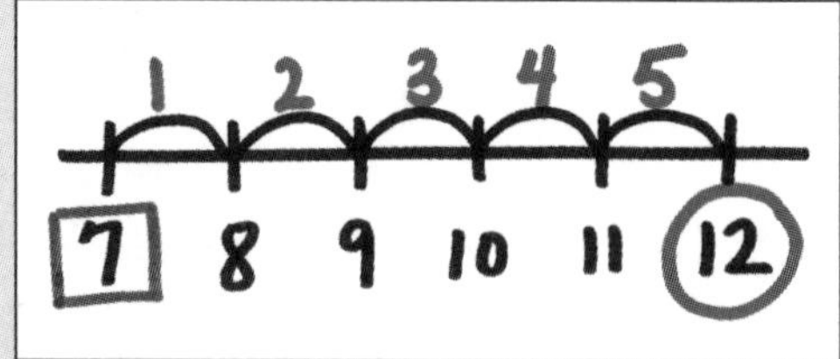

Xavier: Well, I kind of thought about how I could make the problem a little bit easier for me. I broke the 5 into a 3 and a 2.

Mr. Delgado points to the number line on the chart from the previous day, tracing his finger along two jumps on the line showing the 5 broken into a 3 and a 2.

Xavier: I looked at the 7 and I looked at the 3 and the 2 and I decided to start with the 7 and make a jump of 3 because that gets me to 10. And I always like to get to 10!

Mr. Delgado: Okay, I'm going to try to show what you did here, and I'll make a new number line. You started at 7 and then you made a jump of 3 and that got you to 10 *(drawing jumps on number line)*. Did you know 7 and a jump of 3 is 10?

By drawing an open number line in order to show Xavier's jumps of 3 and 2, Mr. Delgado uses a representation to orient students to each other and the mathematics. He anticipated using this particular representation ahead of time because an open number line is a clear tool for seeing jumps.

Xavier: Kind of. I said it real fast in my head, like 7, 8, 9, 10 *(bobbing his head as if making jumps on the number line for 8, 9, 10)*. Ten! But now I know 7 . . . 10, I don't have to say each number.

Mr. Delgado: Let me show the 8, 9, 10 that you're talking about on our number line also. *(Filling in dash marks for 8, 9, 10. [See Figure 3.4.])*

Mr. Delgado: So when you jump from 7 to 10, you're making a jump of 3, and those 3 numbers are right here *(pointing to the number line)*: 8, 9, 10. Let's count those 3 all together . . . 7 . . .

Class: 8, 9, 10

Mr. Delgado: So 7 and 3 more is 10. Xavier, what did you do then?

Figure 3.4 Mr. Delgado represents Xavier's incremental strategy on a number line.

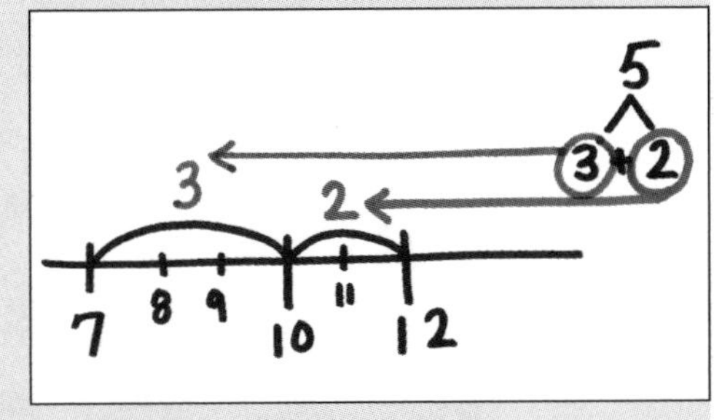

Xavier: I still had the 2 I hadn't used so I added that on to the 10, like 10, 12. *(As he says this Mr. Delgado returns to the number line and draws the jump of 2 to land on 12.)*

Mr. Delgado: So, now we have these two strategies that Keisha and Xavier have shared side by side. With your partner, find three things that are similar or different about their strategies.

As students talk in pairs, Mr. Delgado listens in on several conversations and tries to pick out what students are noticing and how it connects or not to what he anticipated they might notice. He calls on Kenji to begin the connect phase.

Kenji: Alex and I talked about how they both started at 7. We also said you can see their strategies on a number line.

Mr. Delgado is pleased that Kenji is reporting back his conversation with his partner rather than reporting only his own ideas. Mr. Delgado is also listening for whether the pair is noticing the mathematical features of the problems that are similar and different. As Kenji comments about the number line, Mr. Delgado notices a place to probe more. He wants to be sure he allows students to share what they noticed but also needs to orchestrate the discussion so they reach the planned goal of the discussion.

Mr. Delgado: I heard many of you talk about the number lines that are up here. I used the number line to show what Xavier did. Keisha used the number line herself. Before we talk about how their strategies were different, were there other things that you noticed that were the same?

Maddie: Well, my partner and I said that they counted up from 7, and, well, like, I know you didn't ask this but that's also what's a little different.

Mr. Delgado: Thanks, Maddie. It's okay, we can go there. Did you and your partner talk about how their counting was different?

Maddie: Yeah. We saw that Keisha counted each one. And Xavier, well, like he made jumps. He skipped over some.

Mr. Delgado thinks about bringing Keisha and Xavier back into the conversation, and he also notices that sometimes when students explain, they need support in helping describe the mathematical differences. He thinks of asking a question that will help the class articulate why Xavier's choice of breaking up 5 into 3 and 2 was strategic when combining with 7.

Mr. Delgado: *(To Maddie.)* Can you use our number line up here to show what you mean about skipping over some?

Mr. Delgado had drawn the number lines intentionally to help students show how counting by ones and counting by 3 and then 2 are related. Maddie uses the open number line to show how Xavier didn't count each one but counted 3 and then 2.

Mr. Delgado: Maddie and her partner noticed that Xavier made two jumps, a jump of 3 and a jump of 2. Everyone, think about this question: Why did Xavier choose to break 5 up into 3 and 2? Why didn't he break up the 5 into 4 and 1? *(Giving the class ample wait time.)* So, let me go back to Xavier and Keisha. Keisha, before we check with Xavier, do you think you can predict why Xavier might have done that? Share with him what you think he did and then ask him, "Is that what you did?"

Mr. Delgado tries to insert into class conversations small prompts to help students learn how to talk to one another.

Keisha: Well, if he broke up 5 into 4 and 1, then maybe he would have to count by ones, like 7, 8, 9, 10, 11. But we know that 7 and 3 is 10, so it seems like that's a good jump. Is that what you did?

Xavier: Yeah, if I am starting at 7, jumping 3 gets me to 10. So I broke the 5 into a 3 and a 2. But, like, if the problem was 6 plus 5 I would have broken the 5 into a 4 and a 1, because starting at 6 and adding 4 would get me to 10. I always like to get to 10! It all depends on the numbers in the problem, and that tells you how to break apart the other number.

Mr. Delgado: I like how you talked to one another. What we are noticing is that Xavier was strategic in how he chose to break up 5 because of the numbers he was trying to add. So, let's make sure we have a way of thinking about what's the same and what's different. Try to sum up with your partner what's different about how Xavier and Keisha counted up from 7. Then I'll ask a few partners to share what we're learning about the strategies.

By asking students to summarize what they thought was the main difference, Mr. Delgado gives them a chance to stay focused on the main goal of noticing that adding the second quantity in increments that make 10 is a useful strategy. He purposefully invites Keisha to predict why Xavier might have broken 5 into 3 and 2 because he wants to support her mathematically and socially in this discussion. Mathematically, he wants to support her learning about how to add in strategic increments by giving her the opportunity to explain this strategy. Socially, he wants to position her as an important contributor—both for her offering of the common strategies of counting on by ones and also for her understanding of her classmate's different strategy. Mr. Delgado continues the discussion by giving a few students time to help sum up their observations in front of the class. Then, he summarizes the discussion and gives student an exit task so that he can check whether they are able to use the idea in a new situation.

Mr. Delgado: Today we focused on two different ways to solve 7 plus 5. We can solve this problem by counting by ones. We can also solve this problem by making jumps that are bigger than 1, especially strategic jumps that will get us to 10. I have a new problem I would like for us to solve. I want you to try making jumps bigger than 1, and I want you to think about what size jumps to make given the numbers in the problem. *(He poses 8 + 6 to the class, and children begin working.)*

The Compare and Connect discussion structure helped Mr. Delgado's students notice similarities between two addition strategies; from there Mr. Delgado was able to invite his students to try more efficient strategies. We offer the next example to show that the Compare and Connect discussion structure could also apply to the use of mathematical tools. Sometimes students become really comfortable with a particular tool or representation and need to be pressed to consider how a different one works.

Third Graders Compare and Connect the Use of a Number Line to a Hundreds Chart

In this next vignette, Ms. Mason focuses her Compare and Connect discussion on the similarities and differences between a number line and a hundreds chart.

Figure 3.5 shows her planning template for the discussion. Because the open number line can be used regardless of the magnitude of the number, it can offer more flexibility in keeping track of computations. In the case of the problem Ms. Mason poses for her third graders, the hundreds chart presents challenges in keeping track of the direction the numbers are going, because they wrap around from one line to the next. It's important to help students translate

Figure 3.5 Ms. Mason's Planning Template for a Compare and Connect Discussion: Number Line and Hundreds Chart

Compare and Connect

Strategy 1	Strategy 2
Using a number line to compute 82 − 57	Using a hundreds chart to compute 82 − 57

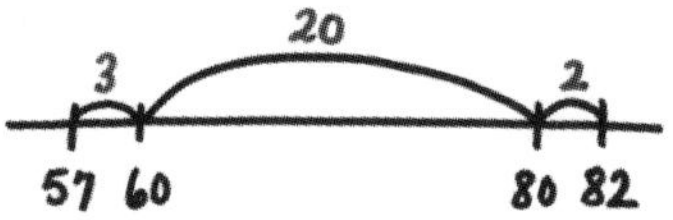

Hundreds Chart

1	2	3	4	5	6	7	8	9	10
11	12	13	14	15	16	17	18	19	20
21	22	23	24	25	26	27	28	29	30
31	32	33	34	35	36	37	38	39	40
41	42	43	44	45	46	47	48	49	50
51	52	53	54	55	56	57	58	59	60
61	62	63	64	65	66	67	68	69	70
71	72	73	74	75	76	77	78	79	80
81	82	83	84	85	86	87	88	89	90
91	92	93	94	95	96	97	98	99	100

What connections are important for students to notice?

Because the hundreds chart wraps the numbers, keeping track of jumps means moving from right to left when going backward. On the number line, you can keep track of jumps on the arcs above the numbers.

Supporting students' thinking

What students might notice	How I might respond to support their thinking
Seeing the jumps is easier on the number line.	How can we mark up the hundreds chart to show the jumps?
You can use the same strategy on both the number line and the hundreds chart.	What's the same? What's different? Which direction do you go on the hundreds chart if you go backward?
The numbers are all marked on the hundreds chart. You use only some numbers on the number line.	How do those differences help you keep track?

What is the key mathematical idea I want to highlight?

The jumps on the number line can be mapped onto to the jumps on the hundreds chart.

between these two strategies so they thoughtfully attend to how they use the models to support their work with, in this vignette's example, subtraction.

Ms. Mason: Today I want to focus our discussion on two different mathematical tools students in our class used to solve a subtraction problem. If we look at the poster of strategies that students used yesterday when solving 82 minus 57, we can see that both Yahya and Simra counted back in order to find their solution. They both started at 82 and counted back to get to 57. Both strategies involved jumping to landmark [or decade] numbers. What was different was the tool they used to keep track of their jumps. Yahya used an open number line, and Simra used the hundreds chart. I'd like to invite both of you to describe your thinking to us and how the tool you used helped you solve the problem. While they are sharing their thinking, I want the rest of us to be thinking about how they used the open number line and hundreds chart and how these tools are similar. Yahya, why don't you start?

Yahya: Counting back makes a subtraction problem easier for me. I like to think about subtraction as finding how far away one number is from the other one. I draw a line. Then I draw the starting spot. Here it is: 82. Then I start making jumps on the line, like I'm jumping backward, and I make jumps to get to landmark numbers because that is easiest.

Ms. Mason: Okay, let's pause here for a moment to use an open number line on the poster to think about what Yahya is telling us. Yahya, will you show us each jump on the poster as you describe it? *(Pointing to the poster where Yahya's open number line is recorded.)*

By asking Yahya to point to the open number line on the poster, Ms. Mason is orienting the students to each other and the mathematics. She wants to make sure everyone understands the way Yahya used the open number line as a tool (see Figure 3.6).

Yahya: My first jump back was 2 to get to 80. Then I made a big jump from 80 to 60. That was a jump of 20. And finally I had to jump back just 3 more to land on 57. That was a jump of 3.

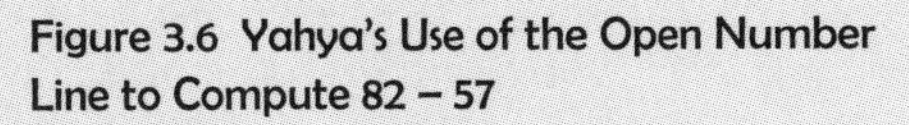

Figure 3.6 Yahya's Use of the Open Number Line to Compute 82 – 57

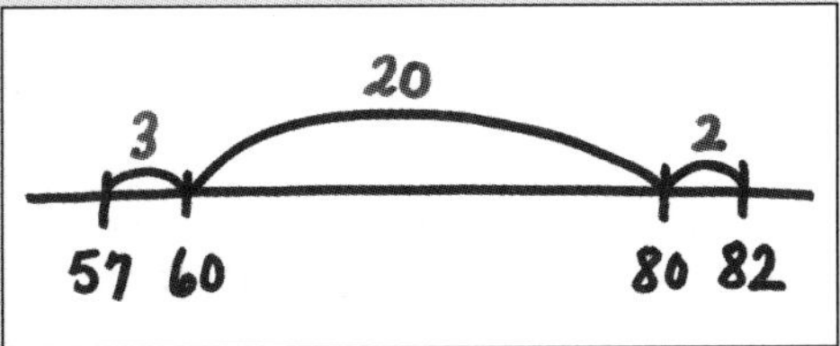

Ms. Mason: So, let's see if we can figure out where Yahya's answer came from.

Students talk with partners. Ms. Mason's use of turn-and-talk invites everyone into the conversation about how to read the number line representation.

Ms. Mason: Who can describe what they heard or said?

Rafe: My partner said that the answer is in Yahya's jumps. She had to add up the size of her jumps to know how much she went back.

Ms. Mason: Can you show us? Yahya, let us know if this is what you did.

Rafe: *(Pointing to Yahya's jumps.)* She jumped back 2, then 20, then 3. So that's 2 plus 20 plus 3, or 25.

Yahya: Yes, that's what I did.

Ms. Mason: *(Turning to the class.)* Who can repeat how Yahya solved 82 minus 57 using the open number line? Maria?

Maria: She jumped backward on the open number line. Like here *(getting up to point to the poster)*, she jumps back 2 and gets to 80 and then 20 to get to 60, and then 3 more to get to 57.

Ms. Mason: Who can add on to Maria's description? James?

James: Yeah, and the answer is in her jumps. The answer is *(tracing the arc of the jumps with her finger)* 2 plus 20 plus 3. Or 25.

Ms. Mason: Can you turn and talk to the person next to you about Yahya's use of the open number line? See if you have any questions about how she used the number line or if it's making sense.

Ms. Mason is using talk moves—repeating, adding on, and turn-and-talk—to support all students in making sense of how Yahya solved the problem using the open number line. Repeating gives all students (including the sharer) an opportunity to hear the idea again. Adding on allows the description of the strategy to be fully flushed out. Turn-and-talk ensures all children try repeating the solution being discussed, and it also allows the teacher to listen in to see if there are any ideas that need to be clarified. Ms. Mason listens in and decides she needs to ask one more question.

Ms. Mason: Okay, I heard you all repeating Yahya's solution using the open number line. I saw you pointing to her jumps and I heard you adding up her jumps. I want to have Yahya tell us one more thing. Yahya, can you tell us, how did you know where to start your jumps and when to stop your jumps?

Yahya: I started at 82 because the problem starts with 82. And then I knew I needed to land on 57 so I jumped until I got there.

Ms. Mason: Thank you, Yahya. I'd like to hear from Simra now. Simra, you also counted back and you also made jumps to landmark numbers, but you used a different mathematical tool. You used the hundreds chart.

I tried to record your solution on our poster but because we are discussing your solution further, I'd like to ask you to point to our actual class hundreds chart as you describe to us in more detail how this tool helped you solve the problem 82 minus 57.

Simra: I will try. I started on 82. And then I counted back. I didn't want to count every one *(pointing to each square on the chart)* so I thought about if I could make jumps that are bigger than 1. *(Looking to Ms. Mason.)*

Ms. Mason: Keep going, Simra. What did you do next?

Simra: I jumped back from 82 to 80, and then it was easy to jump from 80 to 60 *(pointing to the 80, 70, and 60 on the chart and traveling vertically up the chart)*, and finally from 60 to 57. (See Figure 3.7.)

Savion is raising his hand and then jumps up to the chart.

Savion: So you jumped back too. But I can't see your jumps. How big were your jumps?

Ms. Mason: Who can help us with Tavion's question? Simra, do you want to tell us or ask for help?

Figure 3.7 Simra's Use of the Hundreds Chart to Compute 82 – 57

Hundreds Chart

1	2	3	4	5	6	7	8	9	10
11	12	13	14	15	16	17	18	19	20
21	22	23	24	25	26	27	28	29	30
31	32	33	34	35	36	37	38	39	40
41	42	43	44	45	46	47	48	49	50
51	52	53	54	55	56	57	58	59	60
61	62	63	64	65	66	67	68	69	70
71	72	73	74	75	76	77	78	79	80
81	82	83	84	85	86	87	88	89	90
91	92	93	94	95	96	97	98	99	100

Simra: That's what I need help with.

Ying: I see you jumped back 1, 2, 3 *(pointing to 82, 81, 80)*, then 10, 10 *(pointing to 70 and 60)* and then, 1, 2, 3 *(pointing to 59, 58, 57)*.

Ms. Mason: How many jumps is that all together, Ying?

Ying: *(Retracing the jumps again to herself and adding mentally she whispers.)* One, 2, 3, 13, 23, 24, 25, 26. Twenty six.

Ms. Mason can see that Ying is counting the number she started on, 82, as well as the number she ended on, 57, and can see the logic in Ying's thinking. She anticipated this confusion with the hundreds chart and wants to raise the issue of whether you count the number you start on and end on or not. She now knows it is her work to support Ying through her misstep and position her competently in front of her classmates.

Ms. Mason: Ying, can I try that again while you watch? *(Pointing to the hundreds chart, Ms. Mason reenacts Ying's strategy and then pauses, using wait time, for students to weigh in.)*

Ying: Something is wrong there. I think I want to revise my idea but I can't say how yet. I need help.

Ms. Mason: A classmate has asked for help with her thinking. That's an excellent thing to do when you're unsure. Who can help Ying as she thinks through her solution?

Fardosa: It was just so easy to see the jumps on the open number line and on the hundreds chart it isn't so easy.

Ms. Mason looks intently at Fardosa as she shares and uses more wait time to leave an opening for another student to add on. She is using wait time as a talk move to give children time to think and also to bring more student voices into the discussion. She doesn't want the talk to travel through her every time. She wants students to know they can talk directly with one another about their ideas. After twenty seconds, which can feel like a long time, Savion joins in.

Savion: Um, yeah, Fardosa said, like, the jumps are hard to see on the chart. But some of the jumps are easy to see.

Ms. Mason: Which jumps are easy to see?

Savion: When Simra jumped from 80 to 70 to 60. Those are big jumps of 10. (See Figure 3.8.)

Ying: Yeah, I was sure about *those* jumps too!

Ms. Mason: So let's mark them. That might be one way to keep track better. Who can keep us going here?

Savion: It's the jumps at the beginning and the end.

Figure 3.8 The hundreds chart is annotated to show the jumps of 10.

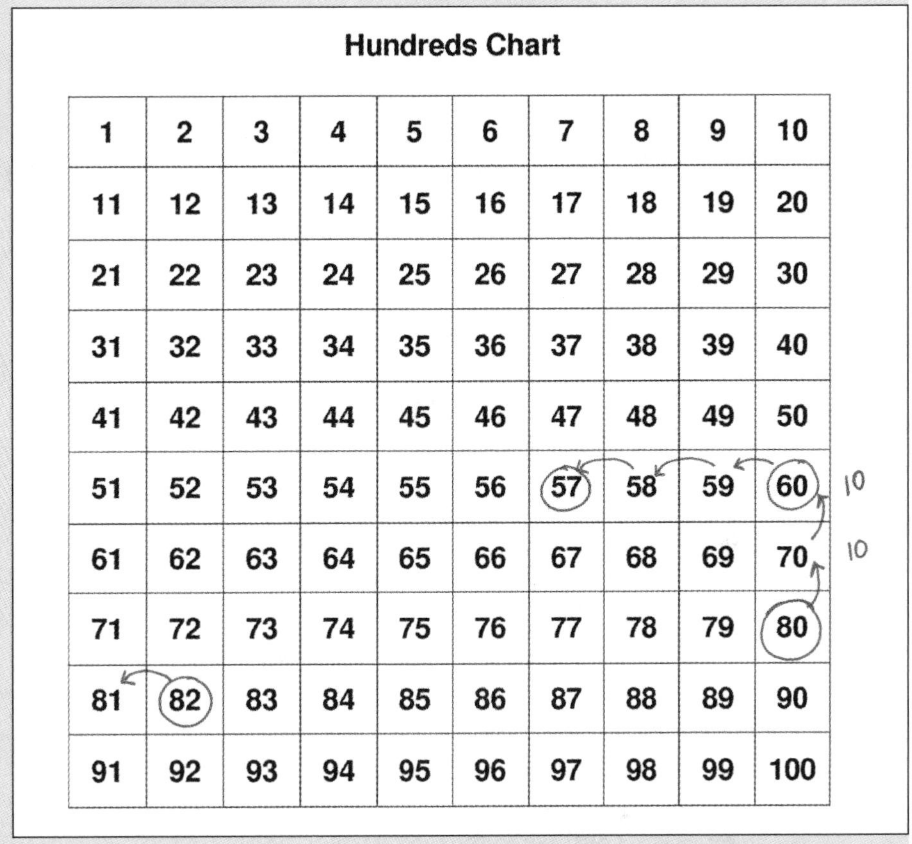

Hundreds Chart

1	2	3	4	5	6	7	8	9	10
11	12	13	14	15	16	17	18	19	20
21	22	23	24	25	26	27	28	29	30
31	32	33	34	35	36	37	38	39	40
41	42	43	44	45	46	47	48	49	50
51	52	53	54	55	56	57	58	59	60
61	62	63	64	65	66	67	68	69	70
71	72	73	74	75	76	77	78	79	80
81	82	83	84	85	86	87	88	89	90
91	92	93	94	95	96	97	98	99	100

10

10

Ms. Mason: Could we look at the open number line to help us think about this?

We leave Ms. Mason's discussions here, and hope you've noticed the careful work she's doing to help the students use one representation to reason with another. It's helpful to look back at the conversation and think about how Ms. Mason used each of the talk moves to create purposeful discussions.

Summary and Reflection Questions: When Do I Want to Have a Compare and Connect Discussion?

In the Compare and Connect discussions shared in this chapter, we can notice the ways the teachers and students focus on similarities and differences among strategies. For example, Mr. Delgado chose to focus on two different counting-on strategies, counting on by ones and counting on by strategic increments. Mr. Delgado focused on comparing and connecting these two strategies because he was trying to support his students in thinking about how they could make decisions about bigger jumps in order to make their counting on more efficient. Similarly, Ms. Mason focused on two different mathematical tools (an open number line and a hundreds chart) that students used in order to solve a subtraction problem.

Compare and Connect is one type of targeted discussion. You may be wondering what types of lessons lend themselves to a discussion about comparing and connecting strategies. You may want to have a Compare and Connect discussion in these situations:

- The problem can be solved in more than one way, and you know, based on your students, that they will have a variety of ways to approach it.
- You want to support your students in making sense of the different strategies that they have generated in order to make sure students don't see the mathematics in the solutions as disconnected.
- You're prompting students along to a slightly more sophisticated strategy.
- You want to compare the use of two different mathematical tools or representations to solve the problem.

Before you continue to the next chapter, reflect on these questions:

1. When do you think a Compare and Connect discussion would be most useful in a unit you are about to teach?
2. This discussion structure could be useful in helping students see connections between their invented strategies and standard algorithms. How might this discussion structure help students really make sense of the notation in standard algorithms?
3. What kinds of anchor charts or displays could you keep after a Compare and Connect discussion to support students' work as you move through a unit?

CHAPTER 4

TARGETED DISCUSSION: WHY? LET'S JUSTIFY

During math discussions, we regularly ask our students to explain their thinking. We know that producing explanations is an important part of making sense of mathematics, and the Common Core State Standards for Mathematical Practice (2012) remind us that students should always be asking themselves, "Does this make sense?" When students reason in mathematics, they develop, use, and justify general ideas about how mathematical ideas work (Russell 1999). They must also ask themselves, "*Why* does this make sense?" The discussion structure we focus on in this chapter, Why? Let's Justify, supports this kind of exploration.

There are natural times in the elementary curriculum when Why? Let's Justify can come in handy, as students reflect on general ideas, concepts, or strategies. Why do you simply append two zeros to a number when we multiply by 100? When can you break up the divisor in a division problem to make the problem easier? What happens when you add two even numbers? Why are four-tenths and two-fifths equivalent to one another? When you are multiplying two numbers, and you multiply one factor by two and divide the other factor by two, why does the product stay the same?

Planning for a Why? Let's Justify discussion requires us to identify the main idea or generalization we want students to examine. We need to anticipate and think through how the justification will sound as students share ideas over the course of the discussion. During the discussion, we need to listen for procedural descriptions that students might give and be sure not to have the conversation stop there. When we press beyond procedural explanations into explanations that include reasoning, we are supporting students in justifying their ideas. For example, if students say that order doesn't matter in addition because that's a turnaround fact, we need to think about how students might use an understanding about the behavior of addition as an operation to justify the commutative nature of addition (Russell, Schifter, and Bastable 2011). How do we plan for a discussion that helps students create those convincing models or explanations? First, it is helpful to consider the forms justifications may take.

Forms of Justification

Students encounter and generate many mathematical generalizations throughout their elementary years. Research into children's thinking has helped us think about the forms of justification that children use when they are trying to convince themselves of an idea. (See Lannin, Ellis, and Elliott 2011 for a nice discussion of mathematical reasoning in the elementary and middle school years.)

Let's go back to the idea of turnaround facts in addition to explore different kinds of justification.

1. *Justification through appeal to authority.*
   Students may justify an idea because someone or something else told them it was true: "My Mom showed me that it doesn't matter what order you add numbers; it's always the same" or "The book says so."
2. *Justification through examples.*
   Once we show students that they can't just rely on the word of an expert, they might try to convince themselves that a mathematical statement is

true by giving lots of examples that work. If order doesn't matter in several examples ($5 + 6 = 6 + 5$; $3 + 4 = 4 + 3$, and so on), then you can be convinced that it must be true. As students become more familiar with our number system, they might try special cases—fractions or negative numbers, for example—to test if an idea still holds. This kind of play with examples can be quite useful for students because it gets them to try out the generalization and be sure they understand what the statement is saying. Of course, examples alone can't necessarily justify that something is true; all that it takes to refute a mathematical statement is one example where the idea doesn't hold. Order does matter in subtraction, because $5 - 3$ is not the same as $3 - 5$.

3. *Justification through a generic example.*
   As students gain more experience, specific examples might be replaced with a generic one. The idea of commutativity might be explored in the context of a specific case, but students might say it wouldn't matter what numbers were chosen: the same idea would still hold. Students may also develop models that help them make their case. For example, to explain commutativity, students might make a model with two different-colored unifix cubes, showing the specific case of adding seven and five. They use the model to show that since addition means combining quantities, the sum is 12, whether 7 is added to 5 or 5 is added to 7. When students start playing with a generic example, they use a specific model but talk about it in more general ways. Students would say they could link together any number of unifix cubes of one color and any number of another color. Whatever the addends, the sum wouldn't change. When they do that, students are using the example of five and seven generically. Susan Jo Russell, Deborah Schifter, and Virginia Bastable (2011), in their book *Connecting Arithmetic to Algebra*, call these forms of justification representation-based proofs, and they are particularly powerful ways for elementary-aged students to engage in justifying claims.
4. *Justification through deductive argument.*
   In mathematics, justifications are always based on logic. When students are convinced by the truth of one statement, they can use that agreed-upon understanding to connect to other statements that follow by logical deduction. So, once we are convinced that order doesn't matter in addition with two numbers, students can begin to extend that idea logically to the idea that order doesn't matter in addition regardless of the number of addends. Younger students may rely on physical or visual models more than on symbols to show the way several ideas logically build on each other.

Thinking about the power of justifying through generic examples can be helpful as you plan for and facilitate a Why? Let's Justify discussion.

Primary Vignette: "Why Do We 'Append Zeroes' When We Multiply by Multiples of Ten?"

Ms. Latimer's third-grade class has been happily working on skip-counting tasks. They have noticed a pattern that the tenth, twentieth, and thirtieth multiple of a number all end in zero and have started to notice that when you multiply by ten, you "add" one zero to the number, as the students say. Ms. Latimer decides to make this a focus of her next targeted discussion. She wants to make sure students understand what is happening when a zero is added to the end of a number. You can see her notes in the planning template in Figure 4.1. On her planning template, Ms. Latimer writes down the representations that she'll use and the questions she might ask students in order to get to the explanation she is aiming to produce. A blank version of the planning template can be found in Appendix C.

Ms. Latimer: Today I want us to gather together on the carpet so we can have a discussion and try explaining what it means to multiply by 10. You have been working on multiple towers and you've been working on finding the twentieth multiple, or the thirtieth multiple of a number. Today we are going to figure out what it means when you multiply by 10. I have some problems we are going to work on. We are going to start with a problem that feels familiar to you. *(Writing 2 × 3 on the whiteboard.)* What does 2 times 3 mean if you put it in a story? In your own words? What does it mean?

Iris: It is 6.

Ms. Latimer: You want to tell us what it is, what it equals? It's 6. Iris is telling us 2 times 3 is the same as 6. What I want us to think about now is what does that mean? What is a situation for 2 times 3?

Tessa: There are 2 roller coaster cars and 3 people can ride in each car.

Ms. Latimer: Wow, that would be so awesome! Can you imagine that? I love roller coaster rides. There are 2 cars and 3 people in each car. That's one way of thinking about what 2 times 3 means. 2 times 3 means having 2 groups and there are 3 in each group. Or, in our story, there are 2 roller coaster cars and 3 people in each car. What is another situation? What is another story?

Figure 4.1 Ms. Latimer's Planning Template for a Why? Let's Justify Discussion: Appending a Zero When Multiplying by Ten

Why? Let's Justify

What mathematical strategy or idea are we targeting in our discussion?

- "Adding a zero" when multiplying by 10. It's not a trick . . . why does this work?!?
- Use a specific example: 2 × 3 and 2 × 30
- Will invite students to generate stories for 2 × 3 and will build on those for 2 × 30

What is the explanation I want students to come up with?
(Include sketch of any representations that might be helpful for the explanation.)

You attach or append a zero (not "add") because the product is 10 times larger.

2 × 3 = 6

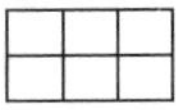

Ten of these will fit in here. It is 10 times bigger.

2 × 30 = 60

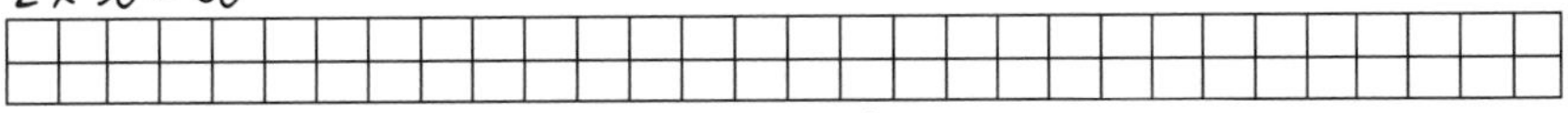

When you multiply by 10, something gets 10 times bigger.
So, 2 × 3 ten times is 2 × 3 × 10, or 2 × 30

Supporting students' thinking
(If students say this . . . then I may ask them this to work toward stronger justification.)

What students might say	How I might respond
"Add a zero."	"If I 'add a zero' to 6, I just get 6. Do you mean append or attach a zero?" "Connect the quantities back to the array model or the story situation. How many 2 × 3s do you think fit into 2 × 30?"

Josh: There are 2 children and each one had 3 toys.
Ms. Latimer: Okay, 2 children and they each have 3 toys to play with.

Since the mathematical goal for this discussion is to be able to generate a justification for why attaching a zero works in multiplication, Ms. Latimer is starting the discussion by inviting students to think through an explanation for a specific example for 2 × 3; understanding what 2 × 3 represents will be an important step in understanding what 2 × 30 represents. She hopes this will lay the groundwork for producing a more general justification.

Ms. Latimer: I'd like to show you a picture of 2 times 3. *(Holding up a cutout array that is labeled* 2 × 3*. [See Figure 4.2.])* I want to know why I can hold this up as 2 times 3. How does the array show 2 groups of 3? Can you point and show us? *(Holding the array out near the children.)*

Figure 4.2 Ms. Latimer uses this array to depict 2 x 3.

Riley: *(Pointing to the array and tracing a finger across the 2 rows of 3.)* Across there are 2 different groups.

Ms. Latimer: Across there are 2 different groups? You have a good idea starting. There is something across. What is it across?

Riley: Three.

Ms. Latimer: Could you imagine that being the 3 people in our roller coaster story example? *(Tracing her finger across the top row of 3, then the bottom row of 3.)*

Riley: Yes.

Ms. Latimer: Or the toys in our other story example? *(Again, tracing finger along 2 rows.)* Here are 3 toys and here are another 3 toys. There are 2 groups of toys.

Riley: Yes.

Ms. Latimer: This array shows that there are 3 kids in one roller coaster car and 3 kids in a second car *(sweeping her finger across each row as she points out the 2 groups of 3)*, or the top row is one set of 3 toys and the row below it is another set of 3 toys. I'd like you to think about what 2 times 3 means and see if you have any questions. If you have a question, you can ask us. Take your time . . . we'll wait.

Wanting to make sure students have a moment to take stock of their understanding of 2 × 3 before moving on in the discussion, Ms. Latimer chooses to pause here. She offers wait time so children can notice what they understand and ask questions if they feel unclear about what they've discussed so far. She waits for 30 seconds, observing the students thinking, thinking herself, and making sure she's supporting the expectation that learners in their class give each other time to think.

Ms. Latimer: I can see you're thinking. Does anyone have a question? *(Pausing for 5 seconds of wait time.)* Okay, it is important that we try to think about what 2 times 3 means. Keep thinking about our story situations as I write out the next problem. *(Placing 2 × 3 array on the whiteboard and then writing* 2 × 30 *on the board.)* So, 2 times 30—what do you think that it is going to be? If 2 times 3 is 6, what is 2 times 30 going to be? You can shout it out.

Students: Sixty!

Ms. Latimer: Sixty. How did you figure that out? Who haven't we heard from yet today? We need everybody's ideas to help us figure this out.

Ms. Latimer uses the phrase "Who haven't we heard from?" in order to draw new voices into the discussion. She is establishing the expectation that all students have important contributions to the discussion and that through wide participation we can reach our goal.

Cooper: You just put a 0 on the end of it.

Ms. Latimer: You're right, I can just put a 0 on the end of it. But can we explain why that works? How can we explain putting a 0 at the end of it? What does 2 times 30 look like? Let's go back to our roller coaster cars. What has changed about the roller coaster story? Let me hear you tell your neighbor what would change in the roller coaster picture.

Cooper: *(Speaking to his neighbor.)* You have to put 30 people in the car instead of 3 people. It would be crowded!

Ms. Latimer: What kind of roller coaster would it turn out to be? A giant car! That's exactly what 2 times 30 means. You would have 2 *huge* cars, and there would be 30 people in each car. What about the toys story?

Calli: Each kid would get 30 toys! Yeah!

Ms. Latimer: And each of these 2 children would get 30 toys. Wouldn't that be so fun? We can see, or picture, 2 groups of 30. *(Holding up a 2 × 30 open array.)* This is an open array for 2 times 30. I didn't fill in all the little squares because that would be a lot of lines. So let's make sense of why this is 2 times 30. Show us where one of the 30s is. *(Kneeling down next to the children on the carpet and holding out the array for a student to point to. Jeremiah pauses to look at the array and then traces his finger along the top of the open array while Ms. Latimer describes what he is doing.)* Okay, Jeremiah is showing us where the 30 is on our open array. And where is the other 30? *(Jeremiah traces his finger along the bottom of the open array as Ms. Latimer narrates to the class what he is doing.)* There are the kids in one roller coaster car and here are the kids in another roller coaster car. Here are the toys one child has; here are the toys the other child has. *(Ms. Latimer now traces her finger along what would be the 2 rows of 30 if the open array was filled in.)* Okay, I have a new question for us to consider now. How many 2 times 3s do you think fit into 2 times 30? How many 2 times 3s are there in 2 times 30? *(Wait time.)* Everybody think of an idea. Think about what is making you come up with that idea. I'm going to ask many different people to tell us what they think. *(Pointing to individual students and eliciting many different answers.)*

Atoosa: Twenty.

Marci: Ten.

Christopher: Six.

Kristine: I'm not sure.

Ms. Latimer: We are hearing many different ideas. *(Recording 20, 10, 6 on the board.)* We are hearing some people are still thinking about this. If you need more time you can add in your idea when you're ready.

Atoosa: I revised my answer.

Ms. Latimer: Okay, you revised your answer. Great. What is your new answer?

Atoosa: Ten.

As Ms. Latimer records all the answers on the board and allows students to revise their initial ideas, she is treating students as sense makers and valuing their ideas. She is supporting children in offering up their ideas even if they are not sure their thinking is correct yet. She wants her students to feel safe expressing their ideas and to know they can always revise their thinking as they get more information.

Ms. Latimer: *(Pointing to the 10 already recorded on the board.)* So, here are our ideas. We think there might be 20, 10, or 6. Some of us are not exactly sure yet. Let's try to figure this out. So this is the 2 times 3 array *(holding up the array)* and this is the 2 times 30 array (pointing to the array on the board). Let's see how many of these fit inside. I'm going to lay our 2 times 3 array on top of our 2 times 30 array and draw a line. We can keep track by counting out loud together (see Figure 4.3).

Students: One, 2, 3, 4, 5 . . .

Figure 4.3 Ms. Latimer helps the class visualize 2 x 30 by placing the 2 x 3 array within a 2 x 30 array.

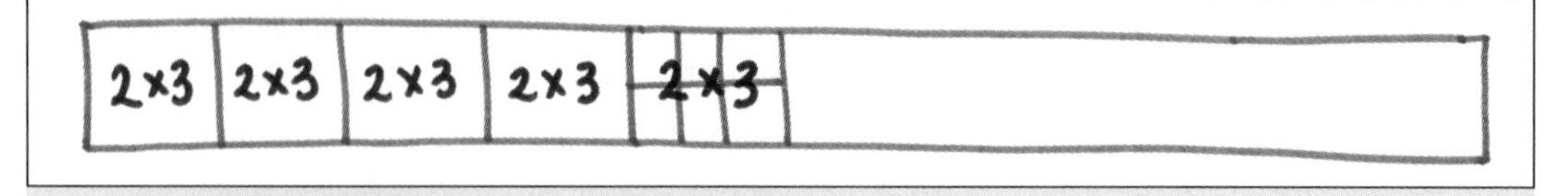

Ms. Latimer: Let's pause here *(the students have counted out five 2 x 3 arrays within the 2 x 30 array)*. We can see how many 2 times 3s we have marked so far and how far we have to go. Does anyone want to revise their idea about how many 2 times 3s will fit into 2 times 30?

Kristine: I want to revise!

Ms. Latimer: What do you want to change to?

Kristine: Ten!

Christopher: Me, too.

Ms. Latimer: *(Looking around.)* Anybody else?

At this point in marking the 2 × 30 array, the students have more information. They can see what has been marked and what has not yet been marked, and they can use that information to make a new prediction of how many 2 × 3s will fit in 2 × 30. Ms. Latimer chooses to pause and offer students the opportunity to revise their thinking.

Ms. Latimer: *(Pointing to the five 2 x 3s they have already accounted for.)* Okay, here is 1, 2, 3, 4, 5 groups of 6, or five 2 times 3s. Let's keep going. Six, 7, 8, 9, 10.

Students: There are 10!

Ms. Latimer: There are 10. Hmm. Now, that is curious—there are ten 2 times 3s in a 2 times 30 array. Hmm. *(Giving 5 seconds of wait time.)* What do you think about that? *(Giving 5 more seconds of wait time.)*

Elliott: I think it is 10 because 2 times 3 is 6 and 2 times 30 is 60.

Ms. Latimer: Interesting. You think that it is 10 because 2 times 3 is 6 and 2 times 30 is 60. If you take the 6 *(holding up the 2 x 3 array)* and multiply it by 10 you would get 60. Interesting. Hmm. *(Giving wait time.)* Did we change the 2?

Students: No.

Ms. Latimer: What did we do to the 3? Can you look up at those numbers?

Kendra: You added a 0.

Ms. Latimer: I did put a 0 there. 'Append' is another way to say we put a 0 in the ones place. Roy, you look like you want to say something.

She repeats Kendra's words to value her idea and then brings in different language, "append," that is more accurate to what happens mathematically when students use this strategy.

Roy: If you do 3 times 10 you get 30.

Ms. Latimer: Do other people agree with this? Do you see the multiplication in this picture? *(Holding up the array for 2 x 3.)* If I want to get to 30, how many of these do I need? To get from 3 kids in the car to 30 kids in the car, we multiplied by 10.

Roy: And to get the 6 to 60 we multiplied it by 10.

Ms. Latimer: You know what you're telling us? You're saying we multiplied by 10. I'm going to write these same problems over here in a different way. (See Figure 4.4.)

Ms. Latimer: We can write 2 times 3 times 10, and that is the same as 2 times 30.

Lynsey: I never knew that!

Ms. Latimer: Lynsey said she is learning something new. Let's all take a moment and see if you can explain to your partner what we mean by 2 times 30 being the same as 2 times 3 times 10. Try to put it into your own words, and let's see what sense you're making of this.

Figure 4.4 Ms. Latimer uses this notation to show the relationship between 2 x 3 and 2 x 30 numerically.

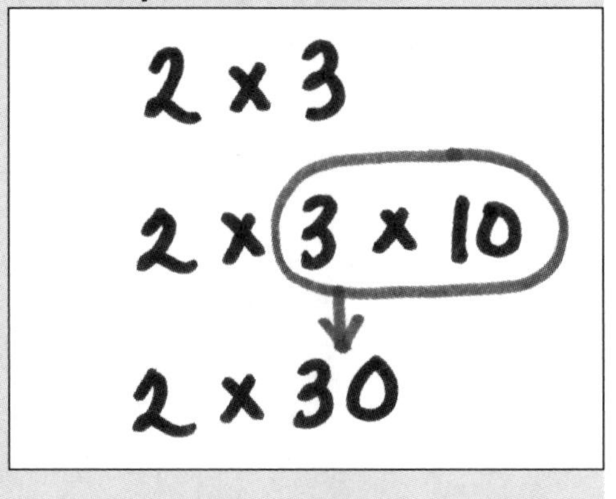

This quick turn-and-talk (see Figure 4.5) allows students to make sense of the idea Roy has just offered. Making sense of 2 × 30 being the same as 2 × 3 × 10 is essential in understanding multiplying by 10; therefore, Ms. Latimer chooses to highlight the idea in a turn-and-talk and give children

Figure 4.5 Ms. Latimer's students engage in a turn-and-talk to discuss the idea that 2 x 30 is the same as 2 x 3 x 10.

a chance to try saying what they understand. As they talk, students can be overheard saying, "Because 3 times 10 is the same as 30," "Because 2 times 3 is 6, but now we are multiplying by 10, which is 30 plus 30, which is 60, and you can do it 2 times 3 times 10. You don't have to do 2 times 30," and "Because there are ten 6s, that's why! That's why!"

Ms. Latimer: I would like you to share some of these ideas in your own words. We are on the cusp of being able to explain what it means to multiply by 10 and why you can put a 0 in the ones place! That is our goal today. If you say to someone, "It is really easy to multiply by 10; you just attach a 0," it sounds kind of like magic, like it is a trick. But it really isn't a trick. There's a reason why a 0 gets put at the end, and that is what we are making sense of today. How come when you have 2 times 3 you have 6 and when you have 2 times 30 you have 60? Let's really listen to your classmate here to understand his or her ideas.

Marie: Three times 10 equals 30, and 2 times 30 is the same as 2 times 3 times 10.

Greg: I would say that 2 times 3 is 6, and that is similar to 2 times 30 is 60.

Rebecca: Like 60 is 10 times bigger than 6. Remember when we counted ten 2 times 3s in the 2 times 30 array? The 2 times 30 array is 10 times bigger. So, like 2 times 3 and then 2 times 3 times 10 or 2 times 30.

Ms. Latimer: Okay, we are hearing lots of good thinking. Rebecca, can you say your idea again?

Rebecca: Sixty is 10 times bigger than 6. We counted ten 2 times 3s in the 2 times 30 array. The 2 times 30 array is 10 times bigger. We did 2 times 3 and then we did 2 times 3 times 10, and that is 2 times 30.

Ms. Latimer: What is she saying? Did you understand Rebecca's idea? If there is a part you're not sure about, you can say, "Rebecca can you explain that part again?"

It can be hard to make sense of complex mathematical ideas and the ways your classmates are thinking about those ideas. Ms. Latimer is thinking about this challenge for her students and she is giving them language to ask for help from one another. She is supporting students in knowing how to participate, especially when they have questions about the idea being discussed.

Stella: Rebecca, can you say the part about 2 times 3 times 10 again?

Rebecca: It's like we know this is 2 times 3 *(taking the array)* and then we see that it takes us 10 times to fill up to 2 times 30. So, that is like 2 times 3 ten times, or 2 times 3 times 10.

Ms. Latimer: Stella, does that help? Do you want to try to say Rebecca's idea?

Stella: Not yet.

Ms. Latimer: Okay. Let me add on to our thinking and try saying our thinking out loud. When we multiply by 10, we are making something 10 times bigger. In our problems today, we made 2 times 3 10 times bigger, and 2 times 3 10 times, or 2 times 3 times 10 is 60. So you can attach a 0 to the 6, because *(wait time)* . . .

Beau: Because . . . it is 10 times bigger! There is a 0 on the end of the 6, because it was 6 but then it was 10 times bigger, so it is 60.

As the conversation concludes there is great energy around the newly emerged justification for why you can "attach a zero." Ms. Latimer invites many more children to say out loud what is happening when you multiply by 10 and take their own try at using words to justify why attaching a 0 works. If a student is still feeling uncertain, she invites him or her to repeat the idea of someone who is feeling more certain. She concludes by posing a new set of problems, 4×3 and 4×30, and challenges students to justify why 4×30 is 10 times bigger and why you can attach a 0 to the product of 4×3 when solving 4×30. As the students begin tackling this new set of numbers, they are testing their justification through examples, the second level of justification, to make sure their idea still holds true with different numbers.

During this Why? Let's Justify discussion, students in Ms. Latimer's classroom were able to generate a justification for why adding a zero works when you are multiplying by ten. It is important to know that sometimes it may take more than one discussion to generate a justification. Perhaps it will take several discussions to work toward a justification, and each discussion will be an important step in being able to justify with understanding.

Intermediate Vignette: Fourth Graders Reason About Decomposing a Factor in Multiplication

Mr. Crandall wants to support his fourth-grade students in thinking about why it works to decompose a factor by its place value when you are multiplying a one-digit number by a two-digit number. He chooses to pose a true/false equation to his students to help them develop a justification for this idea. He anticipates that he will ground this discussion in a specific example in order to lay the foundation for students to explore whether decomposing one factor according to place value will be a viable way to multiply a two-digit number by a one-digit number. Mr. Crandall's planning template is shown in Figure 4.6.

Figure 4.6 Mr. Crandall's Planning Template for a Why? Let's Justify Discussion: Decomposing a Factor by Its Place Value to Multiply Efficiently

Why? Let's Justify

What mathematical strategy or idea are we targeting in our discussion?

$6 \times 19 = 6 \times 10 + 6 \times 9$

True or false?

Remember to ask "Why?"

What is the explanation I want students to come up with?

(Include sketch of any representations that might be helpful for the explanation.)

Choose either 6 groups of 19 or 19 groups of 6. Stick with one interpretation for today's lesson.

Six groups of 19 is the same as 6 groups of 10 and 6 groups of 9—and be able to use the picture to see, understand, and prove why.

Draw picture on the board so that groups of 10 and groups of 9 are in line. This will help students see groups of 19.

Could also draw a picture of 19 groups of 6. So the picture should be 10 groups of 6 and then 9 groups of 6, which makes 19 groups of 6.

Supporting students' thinking

(If students say this . . . then I may ask them this to work toward stronger justification.)

What students might say	How I might respond
"The numbers are broken up."	"How are the numbers broken?" Establish that it's by place value components.
Read the number sentence using only language of "times."	Ask them to use the language of "groups of." (E.g., 6 groups of 19 is the same as 6 groups of 10 and 6 groups of 9.)

Mr. Crandall: Class, we are going to do an activity called a true/false equation. I'm going to write an equation, and you get to think about whether this equation is true or false and how you know whether it's true or false. When I write the equation I don't want you to figure out the answer to it. Instead, I want you to study the numbers and see if you can come up with a reason for why you think it's true or false. Let me give you an example. Let's say I gave you this equation: 3987 + 2365 = 2365 + 3987 *(writing the equation on the board.)*

See these big numbers? Think to yourself, is the equation true or false, and can you figure it out without actually adding up those two numbers in your head?

Mr. Crandall pauses for wait time, allowing children to examine the numbers and think (see Figure 4.7). He's purposefully given them large numbers so that they will examine the quantities instead of automatically computing to compare the two expressions.

Mr. Crandall: Would you do this: Would you check in with the person next to you? Do you have a reason why this is true or false?

Students talk. One can be overheard saying, "It's true! It's true because see they are just switched around!"

Figure 4.7 Mr. Crandall's students use think time to consider a true/false equation.

Mr. Crandall: I want you to say out loud what you think. Is it true or false? Everybody?

Students: True!

Mr. Crandall: I hear some consensus. That means it sounds like you agree that it is true. But *why* is it true? I heard some people talking about why it is true. Why is it true?

Through his questions, Mr. Crandall is pressing students to explain why. Explaining, or justifying, why a number sentence is true is the goal of this discussion. He's made a note to himself on his planning sheet to ask why often during this talk. His students are learning that a mathematical explanation includes why.

Drew: Because you only switched the numbers around.

Mr. Crandall: I only switched the numbers around. And why does that make it the same?

Lynn: They are the same numbers you switched around, and so it would be the same answers.

Mr. Crandall: Who can tell me something about how addition works that helps me know it would be the same? Can we add on to this idea?

Mr. Crandall is noticing that they are justifying the equation by labeling it as a turnaround fact. Listening carefully, Mr. Crandall asks them to think about the behavior of the operation of addition as they try to generate a justification.

Theresa: You get the same answer and you just switch it around.

Mr. Crandall: I'm hearing when you switch it around you get the same answer to the same problem. Here is an example about how you would use that idea about addition: When you are combining two numbers, if you have some amount here and a different amount here and you put them together you will still get the same total or sum, even if you switch the order of your amounts. We are using the idea of what adding means to explain why this equation is true.

Mr. Crandall recognizes that it might be hard for students to explain something that seems so obvious to them. He doesn't belabor the point further, except to provide a very brief example of what he wants them to think about today.

Mr. Crandall: Now that you have an idea of what true/false means, I am going to give you a different problem. Before I do that, let's notice, did anyone tell me what the answer to this problem was?

Students: No.

Mr. Crandall: So for the next one, I don't want you to tell me what the answer is. I want you to think about the numbers. *(Writing the following equation on the board.)* $6 \times 19 = (6 \times 10) + (6 \times 9)$

Students excitedly talk. One can be overheard saying, "Yeah! It is true because 10 plus 9 is 19."

Mr. Crandall: I hear people saying this is true. Does everyone think this is true?

Students: Yes!

Mr. Crandall: Is anyone not sure? It is okay if you're not sure. If you're someone who is not sure, let's see if listening to your classmates supports your thinking. We are trying to explain why this equation is true. Are we convinced by our explanations? Let's listen carefully to how one person starts, and then we will add on.

In order to be able to justify why, you really have to understand the idea. When you are unsure, it can be challenging to know what to listen for in the discussion. Mr. Crandall is explicitly supporting students who may be unsure, or are on their way to understanding why, in knowing what to listen for.

Janine: You broke it by place value.

Mr. Crandall: Janine, thanks for getting us started. You said I broke it by place value. Let's see who can add on.

By offering a student the opportunity to share a kernel of an idea in order to get the conversation started and then inviting classmates to add on, Mr. Crandall is using the talk move of adding on in a unique way. His students know they do not have to have a fully formed idea in order to share. They can share what they do know, and that partial idea can be built upon, or added on to, by others.

Louisa: You know it's true because for the 6 times 9 part you take away the 10 and put the 9 there.

Mr. Crandall: *(Repeating student's idea, then asking a question.)* I want to make sure I'm understanding what you mean, but I'm not sure. Does your idea connect to this idea about place value?

Louisa: Yeah.

Mr. Crandall: Can you tell us how?

Louisa: You make it into more problems when you break it up by place value.

Mr. Crandall: What number am I breaking up?

Louisa: The 10 and the 9 from the 19.

Mr. Crandall: Here is an important part of giving a mathematical reason, a justification. *(Pointing to 6 × 19.)* Let's start with what this part means. Who can tell us what 6 times 19 means? Terrance, you look like you're really thinking. Do you have something to share?

Supporting young mathematicians in justifying their thinking also requires explicit support for what it means to justify. Mr. Crandall is using language all students know ("a mathematical reason") and then the mathematical language they are coming to know ("justification").

Terrance: I'm not sure yet.

Mr. Crandall: Do you want to pass? Do you want to ask another classmate to share? *(Terrance points to a classmate, Grace Marie.)*

Grace Marie: You take one number and you take the other number and you add it that many times.

Mr. Crandall: You said, "You take one number and you take the other number and you add it that many times." Okay, who'd like to take Grace Marie's idea and put it in your own words?

Nina: Grace Marie said you take one of the numbers and you take the other number and then you add it that many times. Like, for 6 times 19, you add 6 nineteen times.

Mr. Crandall: Okay, who else can add on to what we're hearing?

Janine: Or you add the 19 six times.

Mr. Crandall: We have two ideas out. *(Turning to all students.)* Do you agree with these ideas? You add the 6 nineteen times or we can have 19 sixes. We need to pick one of these for our work today. Which one should we pick for this problem? *(Students point to 6 × 19.)* Okay, let's try this one. So if this means 6 groups of 19, I'm going to give you some time to think about this with a partner. We started with the idea that this is broken up by place value. How do I finish this by putting words to what this part means? Six groups of 19 is the same as . . . Put some words here . . . what is this saying?

Pointing to the (6 × 10) + (6 × 9), he motions for the students to turn and talk. He then circulates around the room, kneeling down to listen in on students' ideas (see Figure 4.8). He pauses to sharpen the focus on "groups of."

Mr. Crandall: I hear some people finishing my sentence by saying that 6 groups of 19 is the same as 6 times 10 and 6 times 9. I'm going to challenge you; that's not the sentence I want to hear. I want you keep this language of "groups of." Try again and see what you can come up with.

Figure 4.8 Mr. Crandall kneels next to his students to listen in during their turn-and-talk.

He continues to monitor and then pulls the whole group back together.

Mr. Crandall: What did you come up with?

Dominic: Six groups of 19 is the same as 6 groups of 10 and 6 groups of 9.

Mr. Crandall: Do people hear what Dominic is saying? Dominic, can you say your idea again?

Dominic: I think that 6 groups of 19 is the same as 6 groups of 10 and 6 groups of 9.

Mr. Crandall: Who can repeat Dominic's idea? Jessica?

Jessica: He said that 6 groups of 19 is the same as 6 groups of 10 and 6 groups of 9.

Mr. Crandall: Agnes?

Agnes: He said that 6 groups of 19 is the same as 6 groups of 10 and 6 groups of 9.

By having students repeat Dominic's idea, Mr. Crandall is providing multiple opportunities for students to hear that 6 groups of 19 is the same as 6 groups of 10 and 6 groups of 9, which helps them work toward their goal in today's discussion. He is also choosing to repeat this idea because of the language Dominic is using when he says "the same as." Saying (or reading) the words "the same as" where an equals sign could be placed in an equation is an important part of understanding what equals means, supports students' understanding of relational thinking, and builds a strong foundation for learning algebra (Carpenter, Franke, and Levi 2003).

Mr. Crandall: Let's see if we can draw that in a picture to help us understand this idea. *(Beginning the drawing, narrating what each part of Dominic's idea represents.)* Let's start by making 6 groups. *(Using a black marker, he draws 6 ovals and labels them 1 through 6.)* Now, let's put a group of 10 in each of the 6 groups to show our 6 groups of 10. *(Using a red marker, he adds a 10 to each of the 6 groups.)* And then let's add in our 6 groups of 9. *(He finishes by using a green marker to add 9 to each of the 6 groups.)* (See Figure 4.9.)

Mr. Crandall: Let's see if this drawing helps us think. I want you to look at this picture and see if you can point to where the 6 groups are *(pausing)*. Can you point to where the 6 tens are and the 6 nines? Turn to your neighbor and tell them where you see the 6 groups of 10 and the 6 groups of 9. *(After a few moments.)* Now I want you to tell your neighbor where the groups of 19 are in this picture.

Figure 4.9 Mr. Crandall draws this picture to show 6 groups of 10 and 6 groups of 9.

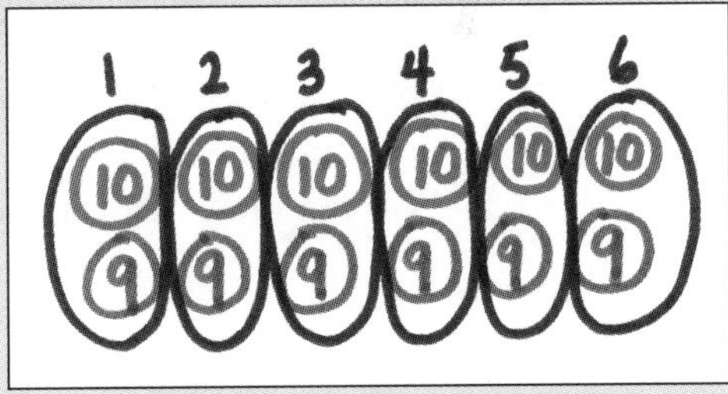

Listening in on the partner groups talking, Mr. Crandall can hear that most students are seeing the 6 groups of 19 as well as the 6 groups of 10 and 9. He decides to bring them back together.

Mr. Crandall: We are creating a mathematical justification. A reason. A reason why this number sentence, 6 times 19 equals (6 times 10) plus (6 times 9), is true. How can you justify that this number sentence is true using this picture? George?

Bringing in a representation and reminding students they are creating a justification are both moves Mr. Crandall is making to sharpen the focus of the discussion and work toward proving why this number sentence is true. With the idea out that 6 groups of 19 is the same as 6 groups of 10 and 6 groups of 9, it is time for the discussion to delve into why these groups are equal, and Mr. Crandall hopes the representation will help support their justification.

George: *(Coming up to the picture and pointing.)* We have 6 groups. In each group we have 10 and in each group we have 9. That is the same as having 19 in each group. So, 6 groups of 10 and 9 is the same as 6 groups of 19.

Mr. Crandall: Who can repeat what George just said? Camilla?

Camilla: He said that we have 6 groups and in each of our groups there is a 10 plus a 9. So that is the same as having 19 in each of our groups.

Mr. Crandall: Do you agree with what George and Camilla are telling us? *(Students use "me too" signal, pictured in Chapter 1, Figure 1.2.)* Why do you agree? Emilio?

Emilio: I agree because I can see it in our picture and I know that 10 and 9 together make 19. And we have 6 of them. Six groups of 19 is really the same as 6 groups of 10 and 6 groups of 9.

Mr. Crandall: So, we have proved that breaking the numbers up by place value makes 6 groups of 19 the same as 6 groups of 10 and 6 groups of 9. You just did your first true/false equation! Did we ever talk about what 6 times 19 is? We didn't have to! We can study the numbers and we can prove why the number sentence is true.

Summary and Reflection Questions: When Do I Want to Have a Why? Let's Justify Discussion?

During a Why? Let's Justify discussion, the talk narrows upon a general claim in order to closely examine the mathematics and generate a justification for it. Certain types of mathematical ideas lend themselves to a discussion that generates a justification for that idea. You may want to have a Why? Let's Justify discussion in these situations:

- A rule or "trick" is commonly used, but students may not have a conceptual understanding of why that rule works and therefore may struggle to generalize the rule with accuracy when solving new problems.
- You can connect a strategy students are beginning to use to a visual model or a problem context in order to make sense of how a strategy works regardless of the numbers. For example, when you want to add two-digit numbers, you can always combine the tens and combine the ones sepa-

rately and then add them together. The model or context serves as a resource for children to verify and test their justification for why the strategy works.

We want to share with you the guidelines that Susan Jo Russell, Deborah Schifter, and Virginia Bastable (2011) provide about how to focus students' attention on justifying a general claim:

1. Choose accessible numbers when first trying to make sense of a general idea.
2. Use a set of expressions or a true/false equation (like you read about in this chapter's vignettes) and focus on the meaning of the expressions instead of just carrying out the computation.
3. Ask students to show their ideas using cubes, number lines, arrays, story contexts, or other representations they have been working with.
4. Identify general claims worth justifying by listening for the patterns, mathematical relationships, or underlying structure of numbers your students notice as they do mathematics.

Before you go on to the next chapter, reflect on these questions:

1. Reflecting on my teaching experiences, what are some of the rules or tricks that I've always wanted my students to make sense of? Which of these might I be able to target in the coming weeks?
2. What generalizations come up as my students develop strategies for adding, subtracting, multiplying, and dividing? How can these general ideas be fodder for Why? Let's Justify discussions?
3. How am I currently supporting my students in justifying their ideas? What are the next steps I want to take in facilitating discussions that incorporate justification?

CHAPTER 5

TARGETED DISCUSSION: WHAT'S BEST AND WHY?

While it is possible for students to solve some problems in many different ways, they also need opportunities to become more selective about when to use a particular strategy. In this chapter we focus on a discussion structure we call What's Best and Why? Instead of eliciting many different ways to solve a particular problem, the teacher structures the discussion in one of two ways:

1. Shows a particular strategy and then asks students to generate an effective use of that strategy
2. Shows a few different ways to solve a problem and asks students to figure out which is the most efficient strategy for that problem

With What's Best and Why? discussions, we're asking students to analyze situations and decide on the effectiveness of particular strategies. The emphasis is not on generating the strategies themselves but on judging when to use particular approaches. Our first vignette takes us into a kindergarten classroom where children are working on ways to keep track of and record their counting. The class considers what is the best way to record their counting and why.

In the second vignette in this chapter, third graders study subtraction problems in order to judge whether it's more efficient to use an adding on strategy or a removal one.

Kindergartners Consider, "What's the Best Way to Record Our Count?"

Ms. Abrahamson's use of the planning template helps her get ready for a discussion with her kindergarten students to develop a recording technique for keeping track of how they count a collection of objects (see Figure 5.1; a blank planning

Figure 5.1 Ms. Abrahamson's Planning Template for a What's Best and Why? Discussion About Recording Counts

What's Best and Why?

What is my goal? What strategy(ies) am I highlighting?

To support students in recording their count by making a symbol for each item with a running total written beneath each item—the next step toward more efficient and accurate ways to record

I want students to think about how writing numbers under the picture of each item will help them know how many things they have counted. I'd like for them to be able to see that this type of recording will allow them to rely on the symbol to know the magnitude of the quantity.

What tasks/problems help us discuss what is best and why?

Counting Collections

- Use poster from previous day to orient students to different ways of recording.
- Select a student who has been writing numbers (like Ange) to keep track and share that particular strategy.
- Ask students to note how that recording method helps someone know how many items were counted.
- Keep chart up in class and remind students to try to use that recording method the next time they count.

What's Best and Why? (continued)
What would I like to hear from my students?
Writing numbers under the picture of each item will help me know how many things I have counted—I will not have to go back and count all the things in my picture.

template is provided in Appendix D). Creating a recording of their count is an important part of learning to form an abstract and fixed representation of the physical work students do when they sort and move a collection of objects.

Ms. Abrahamson's kindergarten students are busily engaged in counting collections. Spread out across the classroom floor, children are counting collections such as bottle caps, puzzle pieces, birthday candles, and glass marbles (see Figure 5.2 and Appendix G). (Counting collections is an instructional activity designed by Megan Franke; see Schwerdtfeger and Chan 2007.)

Since it is early in the school year, the children have mostly spent their counting collections time learning how to count with a partner and keep track of how many items they've counted. They have just begun talking about how to record their count on paper in order to represent how many items they've counted.

Figure 5.2 Kindergarten Students Counting Collections on the Carpet

Figure 5.3 The poster from the previous day's discussion shows recording strategies.

Today, as Ms. Abrahamson walks around the room, she can see that students are using a range of ways to record, and she jots notes to herself on her clipboard. She glances up to the easel where a poster created during the previous day's discussion still hangs (Figure 5.3).

Ms. Abrahamson thinks to herself about how to support students in efficiently and accurately recording their counts. She decides to gather the whole class back together on the carpet to further discuss recording strategies (Figure 5.4). Her plan is to use the poster from the previous day to target the strategy of representing items while simultaneously keeping a running total, a strategy she saw more students trying on today.

Ms. Abrahamson: Kindergartners, I see you are working hard to record your counts. I see you are drawing symbols because we agreed we do not need to draw each item in detail. We learned that mathematicians use symbols to represent items. I want to look together again at our poster from yesterday. Do you remember the different ways students in our class recorded their counts?

Figure 5.4 Ms. Abrahamson begins the discussion with her students.

Seeing that many students want to share, she invites a few children to help the class remember the recording strategies. Then, she repeats all the ideas.

Ms. Abrahamson: Yes! We remember that Gloria and Cayden drew squares. Mikko and Isaiah drew Xs. Dylan and Ashely wrote out numbers. And, Naomi and Samira drew squares with numbers inside the squares.

By recapping students' strategies, Ms. Abrahamson is reorienting students to the mathematical ideas that were shared the previous day. She is also valuing all of the thinking that students brought to the discussion and shows that their thinking is going to continue to help everyone learn today.

Ms. Abrahamson: Do you want to add anything else to what we remember about these strategies for recording? Afsar?

Afsar: I remember that they drew them all in a line. Not aaalll ooovvver the paper! *(Quickly moving his finger in the air as if the representations were scattered all over the poster.)*

Ms. Abrahamson: That's right! How important. When you record the items all over the paper, it is hard to keep track of how many you have recorded. But, like Afsar reminded us, if you draw them in a line, you can easily go back and count. Let's look at the lines of recorded items we see on our poster. Here is a line of squares. What other lines do you notice? Abril?

Abril: I see a line of Xs. *(Tracing her finger in the air as she points to the poster.)*

Ms. Abrahamson: Yes, a line of Xs, too. I would like for us to look closely at the squares with numbers in them that Naomi and Samira drew. Naomi and Samira, can you tell us why you wrote numbers inside your squares?

Samira: We drew numbers inside the squares because we wanted to know how many squares we had.

Ms. Abrahamson: Naomi, do you want to add anything to what Samira has said?

Naomi: We drew squares and numbers. Like, square, number, square, number.

Ms. Abrahamson: So you are saying that every time you drew a square, you wrote a number inside the square. Let's all try Samira and Naomi's strategy together. *(Turning to the next sheet of poster paper, Ms. Abrahamson takes out a chart marker and grabs a nearby collection of birthday candles.)* We are going to pretend we are counting this collection together and recording our count on this poster. Every time we count a candle, we are going to make a square with a number inside of it. *(Holding up a candle, Ms. Abrahamson draws a square with a 1 inside when the class counts "one." They continue for the second and third candle, and then she holds up the fourth candle and turns to the class.)* How should we record this candle? Who can come up and continue our recording for us? Spencer? *(Spencer approaches the poster and draws a square and pauses. As Ms. Abrahamson uses wait time, Spencer's classmates start saying, "Four!" and he writes a 4 inside the square.)* Thank you, Spencer. Let's have someone else come up and record the next item for us. *(Holding up the fifth candle.)* Olive? *(Olive comes up to the poster and draws a square with a 5 inside.)* (See Figure 5.5.) Now I

Figure 5.5 Ms. Abrahamson's class created this poster as they practiced recording using a square with a number inside.

want you to turn to your neighbor and tell them how you would record this next candle and why you would record it that way.

Since the goal of this discussion is to support students in recording their count by drawing a symbol and writing a number for each item, Ms. Abrahamson is choosing to practice this strategy using Samira and Naomi's work as inspiration. By inviting the children to turn and talk about how and why they would record the next number, she is giving all students a chance to engage in a sense-making discussion about why they might record in this way. She is also giving herself a chance to listen in on what students are understanding and decide where to go next. She's especially curious about students' explanations for why they would record it that way since this discussion is focused on what's best and why.

Ms. Abrahamson: As you were talking to your neighbor, I listened to your ideas about *why* we are recording with a square and a number. I want to ask Ange to share what she was saying.

Ange: When we put the number there we know how many things we counted. We count it as we go! Then we know how many we have.

Ms. Abrahamson: Who can repeat what Ange said about *why* we are recording with a number? I'm going to ask several people to repeat this idea. Alex, then Nathan, then Lucille.

Alex: She said when we put the number right there we know how many there are.

Nathan: You can put a number under each thing and then we know how many we have.

Lucille: We can write a number each time to keep track.

Ange has offered up the strategy Ms. Abrahamson wants to highlight in this discussion. After Ange shares this strategy, Ms. Abrahamson chooses to have a few students repeat the idea in order to give students multiple opportunities to hear the targeted strategy.

Ms. Abrahamson: *(Turning to the whole class.)* Do you hear what Ange, Alex, Nathan, and Lucille are saying? They are saying that recording a number inside, or next to, the item helps us know how many items we have in our collection. They are talking about something that is important in recording. They are talking about being able to keep track of how many items you counted by using symbols and numbers. When we use numbers too we don't have to go back and count all our marks; we already know how many we have. I want you to look at our poster and think about how we could use Samira and Naomi's strategy of writing the numbers. What would it look like to add numbers to one of the ways of recording we already have here?

Ms. Abrahamson: Ruby, what is your idea?

Ruby: We could put numbers under the Xs.

Ms. Abrahamson: We could put numbers under the Xs. Ruby, will you come up and do that for us? We will count along with you while you record the numbers.

Ruby writes a number below each X while the class counts out loud together.

Ms. Abrahamson: How many items do we have?

Students: *(All together.)* Nine.

Ms. Abrahamson: We have 9. Do we need to go back and count all the Xs? *(Students shake their heads no.)* No, we do not need to go back and count all the Xs because we can keep track of the number while we count. I have one more question for you. How can you use Samira and Naomi's strategy to help you? Henry?

Henry: We can use their idea next time we are recording a collection and we will know how many we have when we are finished!

Third Graders Discuss Counting Back Versus Counting On

Mr. Soeur's third graders have a nice repertoire of strategies for subtraction. They can think about subtraction as removing one quantity from another or as finding the difference between two quantities. His students have been showing flexibility in moving up and down the number line. He'd like for them to think explicitly about when it might be best to count backward and remove a quantity from one number in order to find the difference and when it might be best to count forward and find the distance between two numbers. Mr. Soeur knows that how far the numbers are away from one another can sometimes make one strategy more efficient than another. He doesn't want to assume that his students have realized this too. So, he uses the What's Best and Why? planning template to help him raise this issue explicitly. (See Figure 5.6.)

Mr. Soeur uses a set of problems from the previous day, when he focused only on generating strategies, so the students already have worked on the computation. The sequence of computational problems, or "number string," is such that the difference between the two numbers in each problem is purposefully

Figure 5.6 Mr. Soeur's Planning Template for a What's Best and Why? Discussion About Counting Back Versus Counting On

What's Best and Why?
What is my goal? What strategy(ies) am I highlighting?
To think together about which strategy to choose when subtracting numbers. Specifically, counting back when numbers are far apart. Counting on when numbers are close together.
What tasks/problems help us discuss what is best and why?
Number string 33 – 4 33 – 7 42 – 37 33 – 28 • Return to strategies from yesterday. • Ask students to think about why they chose going backward or taking away for first two and adding up for the second two. Perhaps focus just on what they did for 33 – 4 and 33 – 28. • Ask students to reflect on why those strategies work in relation to how the operation of subtraction behaves.
What would I like to hear from my students?
When numbers are far apart, it can be easier to go backward from the larger number, to take away. When numbers are close together, it can be easier to go forward from the smaller number, to count on or add up. Either way works because we can think about subtraction as comparing two numbers and seeing how far apart they are from each other or as taking away one amount from another.

exaggerated. He chose problems that were not difficult for his class so he could focus their energies on which subtraction strategy to use and why.

Our work with number strings, specifically adding on versus removing, is informed by the research of Catherine Fosnot and Maarten Dolk and their Young Mathematicians at Work series (particularly *Constructing Number Sense, Addition, and Subtraction*, 2001). We are taking up their ideas about adding on versus removing to imagine a targeted discussion about finding the distance between numbers and engaging in a discussion with children about what's best and why.

Mr. Soeur: As we have been solving subtraction problems, I have noticed two particular strategies you are using often. Today I want to look carefully at those two strategies and think about when you might choose to use one strategy instead of the other. We know mathematicians often have many ways to solve a problem and that mathematicians, before solving a problem, stop to think carefully about which strategy to use depending on the numbers in the problem. So let's begin by looking at the number string we were solving yesterday and remember the two main ways you were solving these subtraction problems.

The Common Core State Standards for Mathematical Practice (2012) have given Mr. Soeur some nice language about how to help students learn what it means to do mathematics. Today, he is highlighting the idea of planning a solution pathway before jumping in, as described in the first Mathematical Practice, "Make sense of problems and persevere in solving them." Also, he is emphasizing the importance of making sense of quantities and their relationships in problem situations, as written about in the second Mathematical Practice, "Reason abstractly and quantitatively."

Mr. Soeur: *(Pointing to the poster shown in Figure 5.7.)* Here is our number string from yesterday. I want you to look at our poster from yesterday, and I want you to think to yourself about the ways you and your classmates were solving and discussing each of these problems.

Mr. Soeur rests his chin on his hand to model think time and waits for a full minute before inviting the class to share; see Figure 5.8.

Figure 5.7 The Poster Showing the Previous Day's Number String

33 - 4
33 - 7
42 - 37
33 - 28

Figure 5.8
Mr. Soeur models think time.

Mr. Soeur: Let's begin by focusing on the first set of problems. I want you to turn and tell a neighbor what you remember about the common way students were solving the problems 33 minus 4 and 33 minus 7.

Mr. Soeur chooses to use think time and a turn-and-talk to allow the students to call up the strategies he wants to highlight. He knows which strategies he wants to emerge and is listening in on the turn-and-talk in order to invite those students who are talking about the target strategies to share. One way to bring up the targeted strategies in a What's Best and Why? discussion is for the teacher to recap the strategies. Another way is to have the students offer up the strategies, as Mr. Soeur is doing here.

Mr. Soeur: As you were sharing, I could hear many pairs talking about the same strategy. Orlando, will you tell us what you and Vivianne were saying?

Orlando: We remembered that lots of people were counting back. Like for 33 minus 4, people were saying they point to the 33 and then say 32, 31, 30, 29. *(Many students are using the "me too" sign as Orlando speaks.)*

Mr. Soeur: Okay, we can see many people agree with what Orlando is saying. Does anyone want to add on to that?

Chaz: Yeah, and people were using, like, the hundreds chart or the number line on our wall to think. *(Pointing to the hundreds chart.)* I point to 33 and then I hop back and land on the 29.

Mr. Soeur: You are saying that people are using tools we have in our room to help them solve, and we hear you saying that for a problem like 33 minus 4 people were hopping back. Let's draw an open number line to see this strategy. We can all count back out loud together and I will record our hops on the number line.

Mr. Soeur planned to use an open number line during this discussion because of the way a number line helps show distance between numbers (see Figure 5.9). One way to think about subtraction is to think about the distance between the two numbers. The numbers in this number string are designed to generate discussion about deciding between using a counting back strategy or counting on strategy based on whether the numbers are close together or far apart.

Students: Thirty-two, 31, 30, 29.

Mr. Soeur: What we are doing is called counting back. Let's do that together again so we can practice what it sounds like to count back.

Students: Thirty-two, 31, 30, 29.

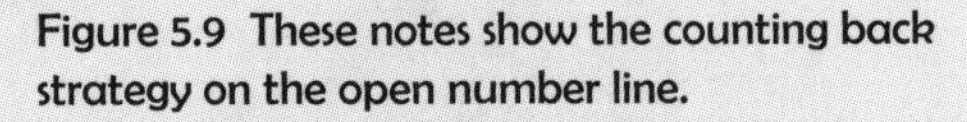

Figure 5.9 These notes show the counting back strategy on the open number line.

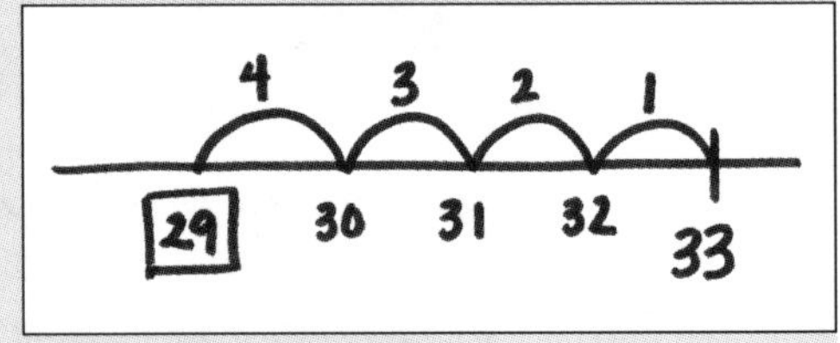

Mr. Soeur: What I want us to think about is why people were solving this problem by counting back. Take a moment to think on your own, and then turn to a neighbor and explain why you think people were counting back when they solved 33 minus 4. *(After wait time and the turn-and-talk.)* What ideas do we have?

Marco: It's just easy that way.

Mr. Soeur: Can you say more? What makes it easy?

Marco: It's easy because you just jump back—just jump back four times.

Mr. Soeur: Marco says you just jump back four times. You only have to make four jumps. Do you agree with Marco? *(Seeing many "me too" signs.)* Why do you agree?

Roshann: I agree with Marco because it is easy to hop back, but I'm confused. The numbers in the problem are far apart, but on the number line they are close together.

Mr. Soeur: Say what you're confused about again, Roshann.

Roshann: *(Getting up and pointing to the numbers in the number string.)* See here the 33 and 4? Those numbers are way far apart *(holding her arms open wide)* but then here on the number line, they are closer *(moving hands together)*.

Mr. Soeur: Roshann, you're noticing something really important. Your confusion is helping us pay attention to something significant in these problems. Who can repeat what Roshann is noticing? Simon?

Since Mr. Soeur's students trust he will support them through their confusions and know that it is okay to share when something is puzzling, students like Roshann speak up when they are uncertain or curious. Oftentimes making sense of confusion is an important step in learning mathematics with understanding. Because of Roshann's contribution, Mr. Soeur is able to move the discussion toward when it is best to add on versus remove when subtracting numbers that are far apart or close together.

Simon: She said that the numbers in the problem seem far apart, but when we see them on the number line they look pretty close.

Mr. Soeur: Another student repeat. Sadie.

Sadie: The 33 and 4 are far apart but on the number line they are close.

Mr. Soeur: *(Pointing to the 33 – 4.)* I want us to focus here. Roshann has noticed that these numbers are fairly far apart. For example, if we look up to the number line on our wall, it is a long way from 4 to 33. Do you see that? You can trace your finger in the air to see the distance from 4 to 33. And if we looked at the next problem in our number string, 33 minus 7, those are pretty far apart, too. But then when we look at our strategy *(pointing to their recording of the open number line showing 33 minus 4)*, we can see we just counted back 4. It sounds like what you're noticing, Roshann, is that when the numbers are far apart, it can be easier to count back. Let's hold on to this idea. Let's examine the other problems in our number string. *(Pointing to 42 – 37 and 33 – 28.)* What do you notice about the numbers in these problems? Zoe?

Zoe: They are bigger.

Mr. Soeur: They are bigger. What else do we notice about these numbers?

Tamar: They are close together.

Mr. Soeur: They are close together. Let's focus on 42 minus 37. Do you remember a common way people in our class were solving 42 minus 37?

Kimberlynn: Well, it was more like people were jumping forward.

Mr. Soeur: Can you give us an example?

Kimberlynn: Um, like, for 42 minus 37 people were hopping forward to 40 and then hopping again to 42.

Mr. Soeur: Okay, let's see if an open number line can help us here, too. Daniel, can you repeat Kimberlynn's idea? I will try to show it.

Daniel: For 42 minus 37 she said you could jump forward to 40 and then jump again to 42. (See Figure 5.10.)

Figure 5.10 These notes show jumping forward on the open number line.

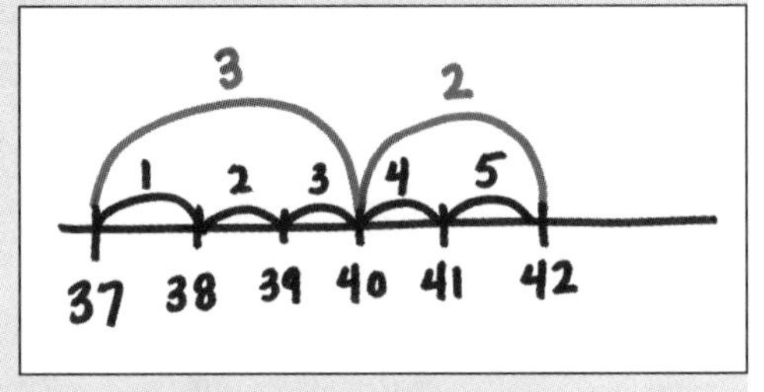

Mr. Soeur: So, Kimberlynn, you were adding on. You added on by making jumps of 3 and 2. And you could also add on by making jumps of 1. When we jump forward on the number line, we are counting on. *(Turning to the class.)* When we jump back on a number line, we are counting back. Today we are focusing on these two strategies, counting back and counting on. When you look at the way we are using these two strategies today, I want you to notice when we tend to use a counting back strategy and when we tend to use a counting on strategy. Turn and talk to your neighbor about which strategy is best for which problem and why. I want to hear what sense you're making of this.

Mr. Soeur uses the turn-and-talk as an opportunity for students to use words to describe what they are noticing and also to hear their ideas and see, as he says, what sense they are making. As he listens in, he can hear many partners talking about the distance between the numbers, using phrases like "close together" and "far apart." He listens further to hear if they were then using what they noticed about distance to determine which strategy, counting back or counting on, was best for which problem. He can hear "close together" and "counting on" often together, and, likewise "far apart" and "counting back" being coupled. He decides for the discussion wrap-up to have children try explaining why they think those are the best solutions for these problems. He asks the class to come back together, summarizes what he was hearing, and asks several children to say out loud why they think counting back when the numbers are far apart is best, and why counting on when the numbers are close together is best. Using repeating and revoicing, they make suggestions for how to decide which strategy to use when they subtract:

> *"Look at the numbers. If they are super close together, then just add up from one to the other."*
>
> *"If the numbers are really far apart, it would take a long time to jump from one to the other. Try jumping back."*
>
> *"When the numbers are close together, add up but try to use as big a jump as you can. You don't have to count by ones."*
>
> *"Think first. If the numbers are close and you want to subtract, just add on from the smaller number until you get to the bigger one. If the numbers are far apart, then just go backwards using the smaller number."*

Summary and Reflection Questions: When Do I Want to Have a What's Best and Why? Discussion?

We want children to have a variety of ways to solve problems. We also want children to be able to select from their repertoire of strategies in order to make wise choices about which strategy to use for a particular problem. Having a What's Best and Why? discussion allows us to target particular strategies. Perhaps you will choose to target a strategy you think is the next step for your students—such as the more efficient and accurate recording strategy Ms. Abrahamson highlighted. Perhaps you will choose to target a few different ways to solve a problem and ask students to figure out which is the most efficient strategy for the problem—as Mr. Soeur highlighted in the discussion about counting back versus counting on strategies. You may want to have a What's Best and Why? discussion in these situations:

- Many students are on the verge of *transitioning from one strategy to another*. For example, students begin to notice a difference between counting up by ones and counting up by tens when adding 27 + 30.
- You would like students to think about *when a particular strategy is useful*. For example, what quantities really lend themselves to a compensation strategy when you round one number and make up for the difference?

(29 × 12 is the same as 30 × 12 – 12. Since 29 is so close to 30, it's a good time to round up.)

- You notice students are getting lost trying to keep track of something and *need to organize information* in order to tackle a problem. For example, what kinds of problems lend themselves to making a chart to keep track of information?

Before you move on to the next chapter, take a moment to reflect on these questions:

1. Facilitating a What's Best and Why? discussion is different from facilitating an open strategy sharing discussion. As teachers of mathematics, we are used to eliciting many different solutions and asking children to explain their solutions, but it is interesting to think about how our questioning and talk moves change when the mathematical goal of the discussion changes. How might the questions you ask or the moves you make in a What's Best and Why? differ from the questions you ask in an open strategy sharing discussion? If it is helpful, you can use the moment when Kimberlynn, in Mr. Soeur's class, shares her solution for counting on by 3 and then 2 to imagine what you would say next. What move might you make next if it was an open strategy share? What move might you make next if it was a What's Best and Why? discussion? Why are your moves different for these two types of discussions?
2. What mathematical strategies are your students working on? Which are particularly well suited to be used in particular situations? Take some notes in the table below to help you identify mathematical ideas at your grade level that might form the basis of a What's Best and Why? discussion.

Idea or Strategy	When is it strategic to use this strategy or idea?	Is this context suitable for a What's Best and Why? discussion?

CHAPTER 6

TARGETED DISCUSSION: DEFINE AND CLARIFY

Teachers often introduce new mathematical objects into math discussions such as tools (e.g., hundreds chart, cubes, protractors), representations (e.g., open array, number line), symbols (e.g., +, <, %), and vocabulary (e.g., parallel lines, product, decimal). As these new objects are introduced, or as they naturally emerge, a teacher must think carefully about how to support students in using them with precision and how to create opportunities for students to make meaning and develop usage with understanding. In doing so, a teacher might plan a Define and Clarify discussion.

We hope you find the Define and Clarify discussion structure helpful as you support your students in making sense of a wide array of mathematical objects that are used regularly in the math class. Our thinking about this discussion structure is inspired by what James Hiebert and his colleagues write about the use of mathematical tools in their book, *Making Sense: Teaching and Learning Mathematics with Understanding*: "Tools can be used to think with. They can make difficult thoughts easier to manage; they can enable some thoughts that would hardly be possible without them; and they can share the kinds of thoughts we have" (1997, 53). Hiebert et al. also pose the question, "How do students develop meaning for tools?" (1997, 53). We take this question to heart as we think about discussions that serve to define and clarify new objects and support students in using them meaningfully. Discussing *how* and *why* to use mathematical objects is an important part of developing problem-solving skills and number-and-operation sense (Jacobs and Kusiak 2006). It is important to consider when Define and Clarify discussions can and should occur (e.g., when objects are first being introduced or when teachers want to help students refine their use).

We share three different Define and Clarify discussions. Our first vignette takes us into Ms. Abrahamson's kindergarten classroom, where children are using a new tool, the two-hundreds chart, for the first time. The class is working with the two-hundreds chart in order to identify and learn how to write a new and challenging number, 101. In the second vignette, Ms. Allen and her fourth-grade students engage in a discussion about the correspondence between symbolic notations, specifically, clarifying how to write eight and ten-tenths as a fraction and as a decimal. In the third vignette, Mr. Tavana and his fifth-grade students use an open array, a visual representation they have used before for multiplication, in a new way to think about how to make meaning of a division strategy for 240 divided by 12. These three different examples will show how the Define and Clarify structure can be used to support the use of mathematical objects, be they tools, notational systems, or visual representations.

Kindergartners Ask, "How Do You Write 101?"

Ms. Abrahamson's kindergarteners are busily counting their collections when Omar exclaims, "I don't know how to write 101!" After talking with Omar, Ms. Abrahamson realizes that many of her students are counting beyond 100, and their current tool, the hundreds chart hanging on their classroom wall, is not going to provide support for how to write these larger numbers. She decides to plan a discussion (see Figure 6.1; a blank version of this planning template is provided in Appendix E), using Omar's question as the inspiration, to introduce her students to a new tool, the two-hundreds chart.

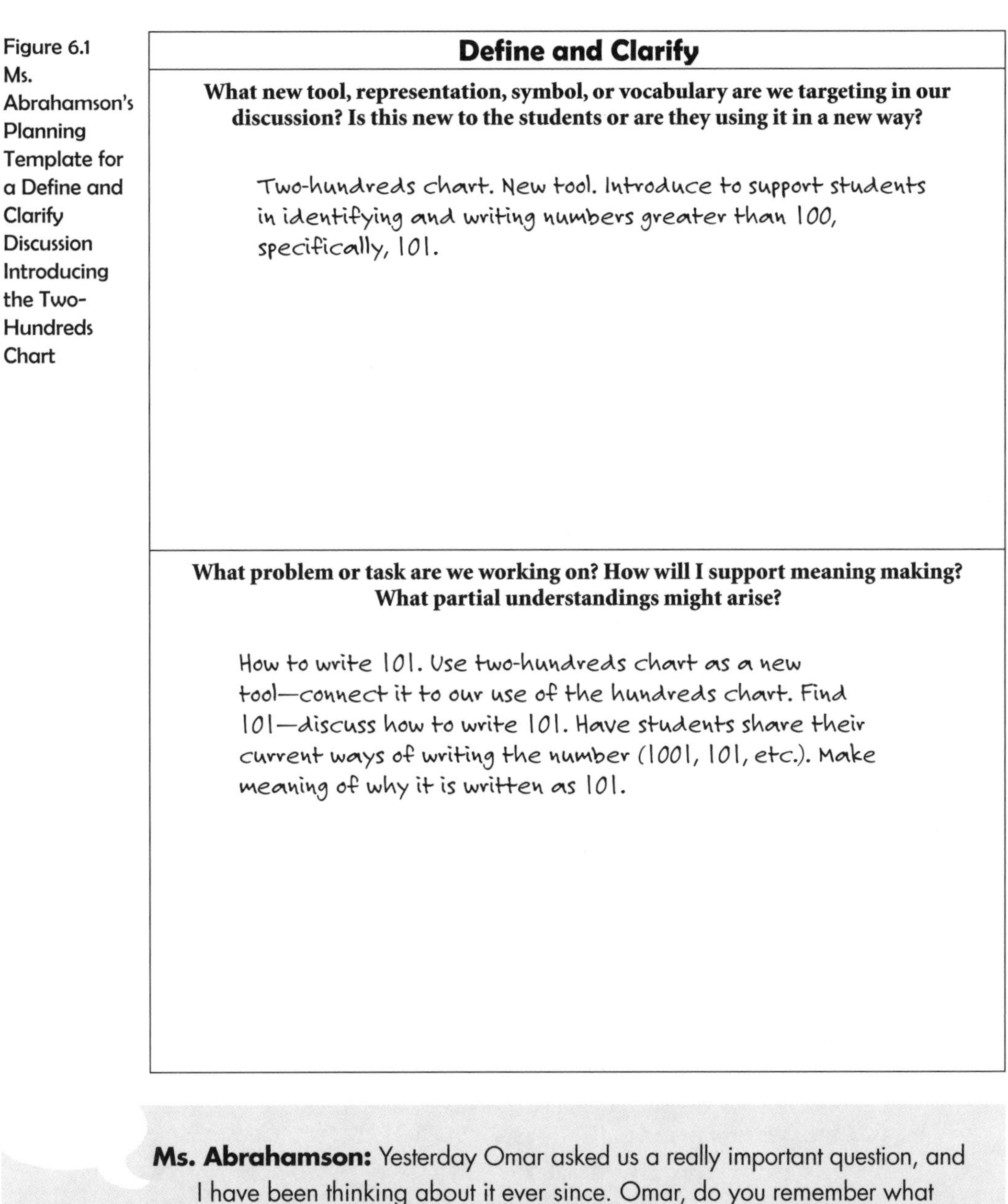

Define and Clarify

What new tool, representation, symbol, or vocabulary are we targeting in our discussion? Is this new to the students or are they using it in a new way?

Two-hundreds chart. New tool. Introduce to support students in identifying and writing numbers greater than 100, specifically, 101.

What problem or task are we working on? How will I support meaning making? What partial understandings might arise?

How to write 101. Use two-hundreds chart as a new tool—connect it to our use of the hundreds chart. Find 101—discuss how to write 101. Have students share their current ways of writing the number (1001, 101, etc.). Make meaning of why it is written as 101.

Figure 6.1 Ms. Abrahamson's Planning Template for a Define and Clarify Discussion Introducing the Two-Hundreds Chart

Ms. Abrahamson: Yesterday Omar asked us a really important question, and I have been thinking about it ever since. Omar, do you remember what you asked us yesterday? *(Omar nods.)* Can you ask us your question again?

Omar: How do you write 101?

Ms. Abrahamson: Do you hear what Omar is asking us? Who can repeat his question? Lucy?

Lucy: He asked how you write 101. I'd like to know too.

Ms. Abrahamson: *(Turning to the whole class.)* How do you write 101? Do people have ideas about that?

Kieran: You write it like one zero zero one. *(Using his finger to write the number 1001 in the air.)* Because it's like 100 and then you put a 1 at the end to make 101.

Ms. Abrahamson: *(Recording Keiran's idea on the board.)* Okay, we have one idea about how to write 101. What other ideas do we have?

Mason: *(Also writing in the air with his finger.)* I think it is one zero one.

Students use the "me too" sign.

Ms. Abrahamson: Okay, it looks like we have two different ideas about how to write 101 that many people agree with. I'll write them both on the board. Let's look around our classroom to see if there is any tool that can help us answer Omar's question.

Sophie: We could use the hundreds chart! *(Pointing to the hundreds chart hanging on the wall.)*

Fiona: We can use the number line. *(Pointing to the number line along the edge of the wall by the ceiling.)*

Students turn their heads to look up at both the hundreds chart and the number line.

Lola: No, we can't, because they stop at 100!

Ms. Abrahamson: Lola, what are you noticing about the number line and the hundreds chart?

Lola: They only go to 100. And we, we are trying to write a number that is after 100.

Ms. Abrahamson: Hmm, Lola says we are trying to write a number that comes after 100. Let's count together on the hundreds chart starting at 90 and look into Lola's idea.

Ms. Abrahamson points to 90 on the hundreds chart (see Figure 6.2) and to each number after it as the class counts chorally.

Students: Ninety, 91, 92 . . . 99, 100, *(students shouting)* 101!

Ms. Abrahamson: I hear you saying 101. But it is not on our chart. Our chart stops at 100. Yesterday when Omar asked how to write 101 I went home and kept thinking about how we could figure this out together. I began to wonder, is there a two-hundreds chart? We have a hundreds chart, but is there a two-hundreds chart? Guess what? There is! *(Students gasp and giggle.)* I know! Isn't it exciting? And guess what? I have one we can use today to help us all answer Omar's question.

Ms. Abrahamson displays the two-hundreds chart with the document camera (see Figure 6.3).

Figure 6.2 The Familiar Hundreds Chart

Hundreds Chart

1	2	3	4	5	6	7	8	9	10
11	12	13	14	15	16	17	18	19	20
21	22	23	24	25	26	27	28	29	30
31	32	33	34	35	36	37	38	39	40
41	42	43	44	45	46	47	48	49	50
51	52	53	54	55	56	57	58	59	60
61	62	63	64	65	66	67	68	69	70
71	72	73	74	75	76	77	78	79	80
81	82	83	84	85	86	87	88	89	90
91	92	93	94	95	96	97	98	99	100

Figure 6.3 The Two-Hundreds Chart That Ms. Abrahamson Introduces to Her Class

Two Hundreds Chart

1	2	3	4	5	6	7	8	9	10
11	12	13	14	15	16	17	18	19	20
21	22	23	24	25	26	27	28	29	30
31	32	33	34	35	36	37	38	39	40
41	42	43	44	45	46	47	48	49	50
51	52	53	54	55	56	57	58	59	60
61	62	63	64	65	66	67	68	69	70
71	72	73	74	75	76	77	78	79	80
81	82	83	84	85	86	87	88	89	90
91	92	93	94	95	96	97	98	99	100
101	102	103	104	105	106	107	108	109	110
111	112	113	114	115	116	117	118	119	120
121	122	123	124	125	126	127	128	129	130
131	132	133	134	135	136	137	138	139	140
141	142	143	144	145	146	147	148	149	150
151	152	153	154	155	156	157	158	159	160
161	162	163	164	165	166	167	168	169	170
171	172	173	174	175	176	177	178	179	180
181	182	183	184	185	186	187	188	189	190
191	192	193	194	195	196	197	198	199	200

Cruz: *(In the midst of many students saying, "Whoa.")* Look at all those numbers!

Ms. Abrahamson: Yes, look at all the numbers. This is a two-hundreds chart. A two-hundreds chart is a tool that can help us as we think together about numbers up to 200. Let's look together at this tool and share things we notice. First, I want you to look at it all by yourself and see what you are noticing. Keep your ideas inside your mind. *(Ms. Abrahamson gives everyone ample wait time. Then, since the room is so quiet because the students are engrossed in examining the chart, she kneels down and whispers what she wants them to do next.)* Wow, I can really tell you're thinking. Now I want you to turn to your neighbor and tell them one thing you are noticing when you look at the two-hundreds chart.

As Ms. Abrahamson listens in on the children sharing what they notice, she overhears comments such as, "There are lots of 1s on there," "I see a long line of 7s," "I found 101," and "The last number is 200." Since she is just introducing this tool, she is curious about what children are noticing and is listening for ideas she can elicit and highlight in the discussion.

Ms. Abrahamson: Let's all come back together. As I was listening to your ideas, I heard many different things you were noticing about our new tool, the two-hundreds chart. *(She recaps many different ideas and then narrows the discussion.)* I heard Logan say the last number is 200. Logan, can you point to the 200 for us? *(Logan approaches the screen and points to 200).* Do you see the 200 Logan is pointing to? Let's all say these numbers together. Two zero zero. A 200 is written two zero zero. Let's write 200 in the air. *(Students write the numbers 2-0-0 in the air.)* Yes! This chart has a 200 on it. It is our two-hundreds chart. There are 200 numbers on our chart. I heard another comment. I heard Adelia say that she found 101. Do you remember Omar's question? Omar, what was your question?

Omar: How do you write 101?

Ms. Abrahamson: Because of Omar's good question, we now have a new tool that can help us know how to write numbers. Adelia, can you come point to where you see 101? *(Adelia comes up to the screen and points to 101.)* Do you see the number Adelia is pointing to? How do we know this is 101? Carlos?

Carlos: It has a 1 in it.

Ms. Abrahamson: It has a 1 in it. Who else has an idea? Paya?

Paya: It comes after 100.

Ms. Abrahamson: it comes after 100. Let's think about what Paya is telling us. I have a two-hundreds chart for each of you to hold. When you get your chart, I want you to point to where you see 101. *(Passing out an individual two-hundreds chart printed on cardstock to each child. Children start pointing to where they see 101 and showing their classmates.)* I want us to count out loud again together and point to each number on our two-hundreds chart as we say that number. Let's begin at 90. *(Counting out loud and pointing.)* Ninety, 91, 92, 93 . . . 99, 100, 101. Stop! Let's stop. We just counted 100, 101. Yes, Paya, 101 comes after 100. And, Omar, what do you notice about how 101 is written?

Omar: *(Pointing to his two-hundreds chart.)* One zero one.

Ms. Abrahamson: We hear Omar saying 101 is written one zero one. Let's all write 101 in the air. *(Students draw in the air.)*

Yasamin: *(Pointing to 101.)* That way of writing it on the board is right.

Keiran: Uh-oh, I want to revise my thinking. I change my mind to think it is written one zero one. *(He goes to the board and crosses out 1001.)*

Ms. Abrahamson: Yasamin is noticing that one of our predictions was true. You write one hundred one as 101. And Keiran is doing something that mathematicians do, he is revising his thinking after getting more information. After using the two-hundreds chart as a tool, Keiran now thinks one hundred one is written 101. Keiran, that is exactly what this tool is for. This two-hundreds chart is a tool we now have in our classroom to help us know how to write our numbers. I have a *big* two-hundreds chart I am going to put up here on our wall right next to the hundreds chart. *And* we are going to learn many other important uses for this tool. Nice thinking, kindergartners. We all know how to write 101!

Fourth Graders Ask, "Is Eight and Ten-tenths Written as 8.10 or 9?"

As the fourth-grade students in Ms. Allen's classroom are thinking about tenths, an important question arises: Is eight and ten-tenths written as 8.10 or 9? In order to support her students in clarifying the use of symbolic notations, specifically, the correspondence between symbolic systems for fractions and decimals, Ms. Allen plans a Define and Clarify discussion (see Figure 6.4).

Figure 6.4 Ms. Allen's Planning Template for a Define and Clarify Discussion on Decimal Notation

Define and Clarify
What new tool, representation, symbol, or vocabulary are we targeting in our discussion? Is this new to the students or are they using it in a new way? How to write 8 10/10 as a decimal. Use the idea of 10/10 = 1 to make sense of why the number is not written 8.10 but instead is written 9.0.
What problem or task are we working on? How will I support meaning making? What misconceptions might arise? Is 8 10/10 written like 8.10 or 9? (Question raised by students.) Return to 10K representation and story context to support making meaning of how to write 10/10. $\frac{1}{10}$ (×20 jumps) 8k $8\frac{1}{10}$ $8\frac{2}{10}$ $8\frac{3}{10}$ $8\frac{4}{10}$ $8\frac{5}{10}$ $8\frac{6}{10}$ $8\frac{7}{10}$ $8\frac{8}{10}$ $8\frac{9}{10}$ 9k $9\frac{1}{10}$ $9\frac{2}{10}$ $9\frac{3}{10}$ $9\frac{4}{10}$ $9\frac{5}{10}$ $9\frac{6}{10}$ $9\frac{7}{10}$ $9\frac{8}{10}$ $9\frac{9}{10}$ 10k Finish Line $8\frac{1}{10}$ $8\frac{2}{10}$ $8\frac{3}{10}$ $8\frac{4}{10}$ $8\frac{5}{10}$ $8\frac{6}{10}$ $8\frac{7}{10}$ $8\frac{8}{10}$ $8\frac{9}{10}$ $8\frac{10}{10}$ 8.1 8.2 8.3 8.4 8.5 8.6 8.7 8.8 8.9 8.10 9

Ms. Allen: Okay, everybody, let's gather together to help each other make sense of a new way we are writing and recording fractions and decimals. Come on up to the carpet. Remember how we were talking about how I am becoming a runner and I have a goal of running in a 10K, or 10 kilometers? *(Smiling.)* I know some of you think that is funny! And remember how right now I can run about 8K, and my friends who are runners helped me learn that I can try running a little bit farther every day—a tenth of a kilometer longer each day—and you figured out that after going out for 20 more runs I will meet my goal! After our discussion, I was thinking more about your ideas about fractions and decimals, and today I want to zoom in on a few ideas, a few questions actually, to make sure we all are feeling clear about how to write tenths as fractions and as decimals. To help us get started, I want to look again at the representation we made (see Figure 6.5). Who can offer up some ideas to help us remember how this representation was helping us think about tenths? Saundra?

Figure 6.5 The class used this representation to count by tenths from 8 to 10 in a prior classroom discussion.

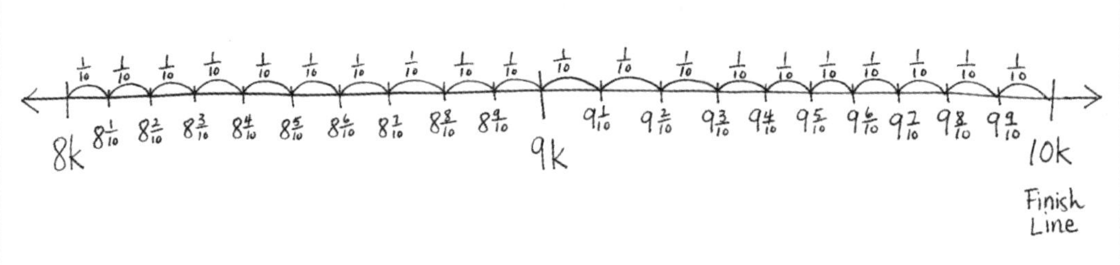

Saundra: You can run all the way to here right now *(pointing to the 8K)*, but you want to be able to run to here *(pointing to the 10K)*, and we were figuring out how much farther you need to go.

Ms. Allen: Saundra has gotten us started. Who can add on to what she is saying? Nicole?

Nicole: *(Pointing to the tenths.)* And each of these little parts is $\frac{1}{10}$ of a kilometer. It goes like $8\frac{1}{10}$, $8\frac{2}{10}$, $8\frac{3}{10}$.

Ms. Allen: So, each of these little parts *(pointing to $\frac{1}{10}$ of a kilometer)* represents $\frac{1}{10}$ of a kilometer, because we divided a kilometer into 10 lengths.

Meghan: And the lengths have to be the same size.

Ms. Allen: And the lengths have to be the same size. Yes. A tenth was one of 10 equal parts in each kilometer. Let's count them out loud together like Nicole started to do.

Students: Eight and $\frac{1}{10}$, $8\frac{2}{10}$, $8\frac{3}{10}$, . . . $8\frac{9}{10}$, and $8\frac{10}{10}$.

Ms. Allen: It seems you're pretty comfortable counting by tenths and recording it this way—as fractions. Mathematicians write $\frac{10}{10}$ as a fraction *(pointing to $\frac{10}{10}$)*. Mathematicians also write $\frac{10}{10}$ as a decimal *(pointing to the row of decimals recorded beneath the representation)*, and here we can see how we also recorded this count in decimals. We agreed that $\frac{1}{10}$ written as a decimal looks like 0.1. This *(pointing to the decimal point)* is called the decimal point. Ten-tenths represents the same portion whether it is written as a fraction or a decimal.

The goal of this discussion is to make sure all students feel comfortable knowing how to write tenths as fractions and as decimals (see Figure 6.6). Defining and clarifying the correspondence between these symbolic systems is at the center of Ms. Allen's thinking as she facilitates this discussion. She is paying close attention to her language and is being explicit in how she talks about the ways mathematicians use symbols and words to represent tenths.

Figure 6.6 This representation compares fraction notation to decimal notation.

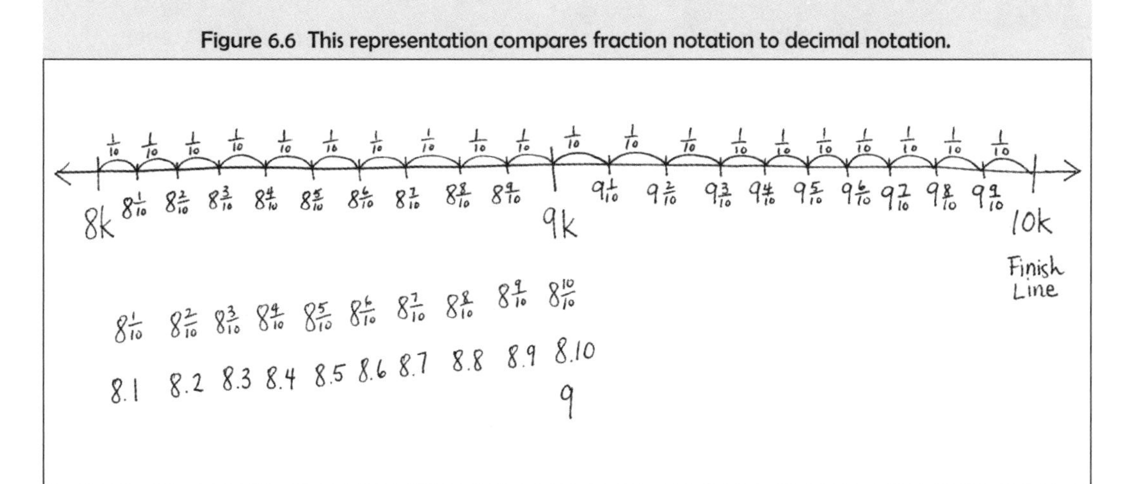

Ms. Allen: What really struck me during our conversation yesterday was a question that emerged. There was a lot of buzzing about how we should write $8\frac{10}{10}$ as a decimal. The two most common ideas were 8.10 and 9. Today I want us to talk together and reason about how we should write this. Our question is: Is $8\frac{10}{10}$ written like 8.10 or 9? And we need to get clear about this together. First, I would like for you to look at our representation and think to yourself about which number you would like to defend. *(After about 30 seconds of wait time.)* Terrance?

Terrance: Nine or 9.0.

Ms. Allen: Let's listen to why Terrance wants to defend 9.

Terrance: *(Walking up to the board.)* There could be a decimal point right here *(pointing to the space to the right of the 9)*, and then because the 9 would be in front of the decimal point, it means it is a whole, and if the 9 is behind the decimal point it means it is a tenth.

Ms. Allen: You are paying attention to the digit that is before and after the decimal. You are saying that the digit before the decimal is ones and after the decimal is tenths. I see people using our "me too" sign. Who else would like to defend 9? Thomasina?

Thomasina: I think it is 9 because it is not 8.10.

Ms. Allen: Say more about why you think it is not 8.10.

Thomasina: Because, um, 8.10 is going to be into the hundredths. Because the zero is in the hundredths spot.

Ms. Allen: *(Pausing with wait time before continuing.)* Anybody else want to add to that?

Ms. Allen can see her students are thinking and she wants more of them to jump into the discussion with their ideas. She is pulling back a bit here to give think time and airtime for students to join in. She chooses between repeating the ideas Terrance and Thomasina have offered or giving a prompt for more student voices. Because there is more to elaborate here she is leaving the door open for more student voices to weigh in.

Alisa: I'm confused. I was going to defend 8.10 but now I'm not sure. It seems like it should go 8 point 9 and then 8 point 10, because that sounds like $8\frac{10}{10}$.

Ms. Allen: Okay, it sounds like you're thinking about what you are hearing. Do you want to share what is confusing you or do you want more think time?

Alisa: More think time.

Ms. Allen: Okay. Who else has an idea to share? We have heard some support for 9. We have heard some people may be unsure or may be changing their thinking. Is there anyone who would like to defend 8.10? We are trying to clarify how to write $8\frac{10}{10}$ as a decimal. What do you think, Kurt?

Kurt: Well, I was just thinking that we learned that $\frac{10}{10}$ is equal to a whole. But 8 point 10 looks like 8 point 1.

Thomasina: Oh, oh. Yeah, I see what Kurt is saying. It's like $8\frac{10}{10}$ is like 8 and 1 whole. So doesn't that mean it's 9?

Ms. Allen: What do you think of what Thomasina and Kurt are saying, Alisa?

Ms. Allen's decision to go back to Alisa is intentional here. She regularly looks for opportunities for students to make their puzzlements more public, to show that wrestling with ideas is an important part of doing mathematics.

Alisa: I think I need to hear that again. It's starting to make sense.

Thomasina gets up to go to the board and gets an approving nod from Ms. Allen.

Thomasina: See, like if we write 8 and $\frac{10}{10}$ like a fraction, like this, $8\frac{10}{10}$, we can cross out the $\frac{10}{10}$ and make it a 1. Then we have 8 and 1, which is 9.

Alisa: Oohh! That makes sense.

Ms. Allen: Whenever we think we're on the verge of understanding something, it's always good to check with your neighbor and see if you have questions about what's happening.

Ms. Allen uses a turn-and-talk at this point to make sure she doesn't assume that everyone listening has developed the insight that Alisa has with Thomasina's explanation. She leans in on Alisa and her partner to check on what Alisa thinks she understands. Students can ask each other questions and spread ideas during a turn-and-talk. Ms. Allen listens in and sees that students are picking up on the idea of the equivalency between $\frac{10}{10}$ and 1.

Ms. Allen: So I think we've achieved a good point of clarification. Even though it's tempting to think that 8.10 says $8\frac{10}{10}$, we've convinced ourselves that $8\frac{10}{10}$ is equivalent to 9 and needs to be written 9.0 as a decimal. I want to go back to an idea that we heard earlier—that 8.1 and 8.10 seem to be the same thing. I'll let you chew on this a bit more. I'm interested in your thoughts on this, so I think I'll let you write about it in your math journals first before we talk about it together.

Fifth Graders Discuss Using an Open Array in a Different Way

Mr. Tavana can see that his fifth-grade students are using what they know about groups of ten to solve division problems with bigger numbers. When thinking about 240 divided by 12, students are using 10 groups of 12 and then 10 more groups of 12 to get to 240. He thinks an open array could support students in making meaning of this strategy and plans for a Define and Clarify discussion to introduce using the open array as a tool for solving division problems and keeping track of a multiplying-up strategy (see Figure 6.7).

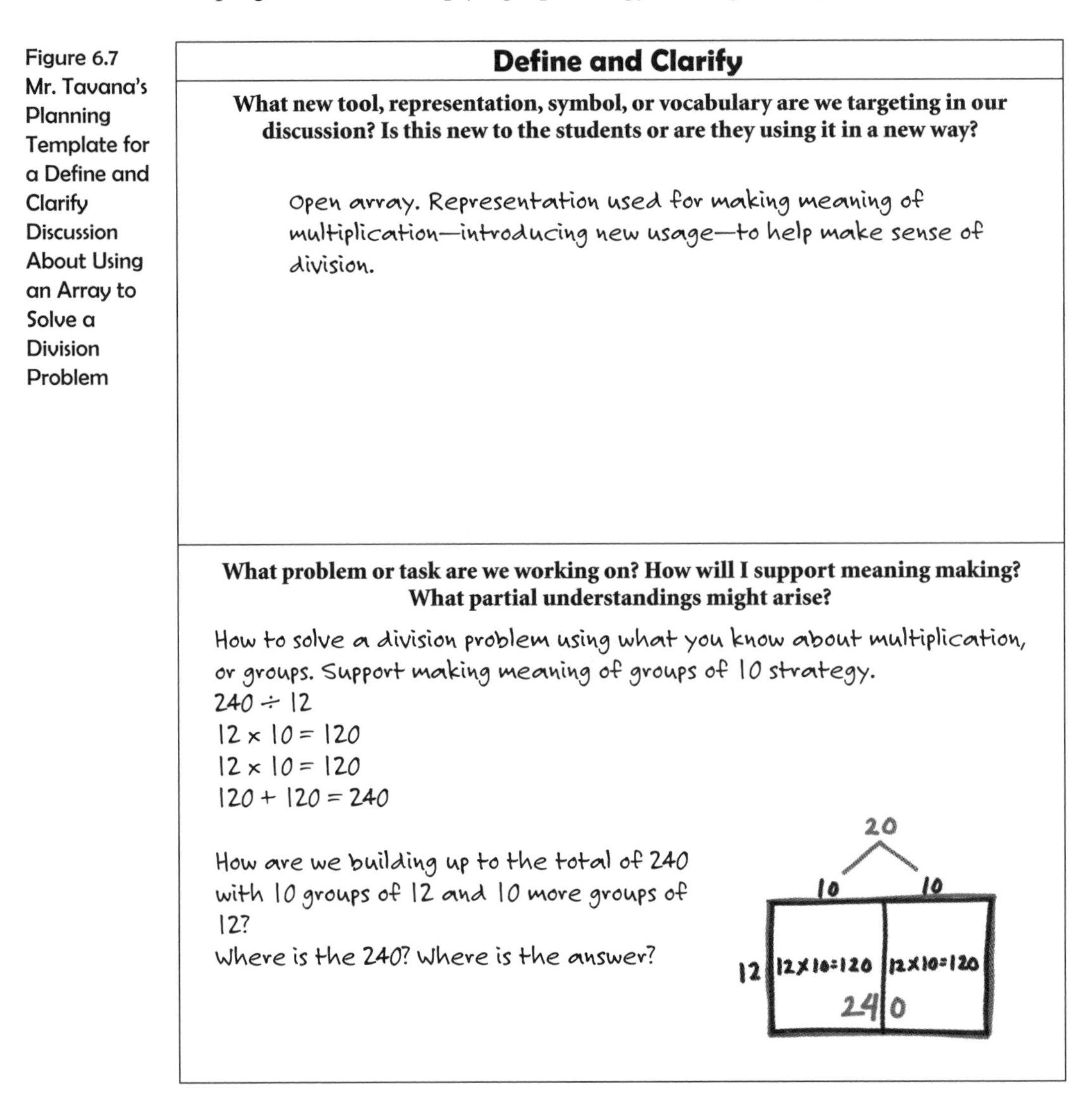

Define and Clarify

What new tool, representation, symbol, or vocabulary are we targeting in our discussion? Is this new to the students or are they using it in a new way?

Open array. Representation used for making meaning of multiplication—introducing new usage—to help make sense of division.

What problem or task are we working on? How will I support meaning making? What partial understandings might arise?

How to solve a division problem using what you know about multiplication, or groups. Support making meaning of groups of 10 strategy.

240 ÷ 12
12 × 10 = 120
12 × 10 = 120
120 + 120 = 240

How are we building up to the total of 240 with 10 groups of 12 and 10 more groups of 12?
Where is the 240? Where is the answer?

Figure 6.7 Mr. Tavana's Planning Template for a Define and Clarify Discussion About Using an Array to Solve a Division Problem

Mr. Tavana: *(Turning to his students, who are gathered on the carpet.)* The last few days, as we have been solving division problems, I have noticed that students in our class are using what they know about multiplication to think about division.

Pointing to the poster on an easel from yesterday's open strategy share discussion, Mr. Tavana focuses on a particular strategy he saw students using for 240 divided by 12 (see Figure 6.8).

Mr. Tavana: After we discussed this strategy of using 12 groups of 10, or 10 groups of 12, to build up to 240 yesterday, I wondered if building an open array could help us make sense of using multiplication, or groups, to think about division. Today I want to talk about how to use an open array, and I also want to clarify how we use this representation to help us think about division. Since people solved 240 divided by 12 in a few different ways, let's start by making sure we all understand the strategy we are focusing on today. Who was using this strategy and will explain it to us? Bethany?

Figure 6.8 This portion of the poster shows a representation of multiplying up to solve 240 ÷ 12.

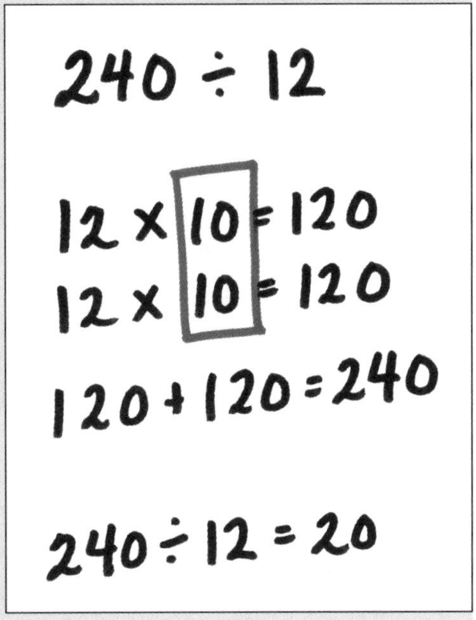

240 ÷ 12

12 × 10 = 120
12 × 10 = 120
120 + 120 = 240

240 ÷ 12 = 20

Bethany: I like to use tens because they are easy for me. So I know that 10 groups of 12 is 120. I thought 12 times 10 equals 120, and then I needed to do that one more time to get to 240.

Mr. Tavana: Who else used this strategy and can add on to what Bethany has told us? Sam?

Sam: I thought about it the same as Bethany. It's like 12 ten times is 120. And 120 plus 120 gets me all the way to 240.

Mr. Tavana: Can someone who did not use this strategy repeat what Bethany and Sam are telling us? Laretha?

Laretha: They used what they know about groups of 10 to figure out how many 12s are in 240. They did a chunk of ten 12s and that is 120 and then another chunk of ten 12s and that got them to 240.

Mr. Tavana: It sounds like we are all grasping this solution. Just to make sure, can you turn to your neighbor and explain this strategy? If you notice it is challenging to explain, ask your partner or me for help.

Mr. Tavana wants to make sure every student understands this strategy, since it was not the way every child previously solved 240 divided by 12. He uses a turn-and-talk to offer students the chance to explain this strategy aloud and ask for help if needed. He also uses the turn-and-talk to listen in and quickly make sure there are not any lingering questions before moving on to more discussion about making sense of this solution through an open array. He kneels down next to a few students to check in and then decides it is okay to move on. Before calling the group back together, he moves the strategy poster from the easel to the whiteboard to make sure it is visible while they move into a discussion of the open array.

Mr. Tavana: We have used an open array before to help us think about multiplication. We can also use an open array to help us think about division. But, we use the open array in a different way when we are using it for division problems. Today I want to focus on using an open array to help us think about what is happening in this division strategy. *(Approaching the easel.)* Remember, an open array does not have all the marks drawn inside. It is a quick way for us to draw areas. I will think out loud as I get us started, and then I want to see what your ideas are about continuing our open array. Let's start with 12 down here *(drawing a line down)* since we know we are dividing by 12. And since students are using what they know about 10 groups of 12, let's show 10 groups of 12 by drawing 10 across here *(drawing a line across)*. Then we can make an open array that is 12 times 10 and label inside that 12 times 10 equals 120. (See Figure 6.9.) Let's check back with our strategy that is recorded on the poster. Which part of the solution have we shown in this open array?

Clint: We have shown one of the 12 times 10s.

Mr. Tavana: Clint, can you point for us to the 12 times 10 on our strategy poster? *(Clint points to the first 12 × 10 in Figure 6.8.)* Okay, so this

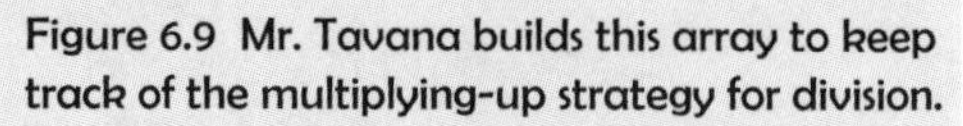

Figure 6.9 Mr. Tavana builds this array to keep track of the multiplying-up strategy for division.

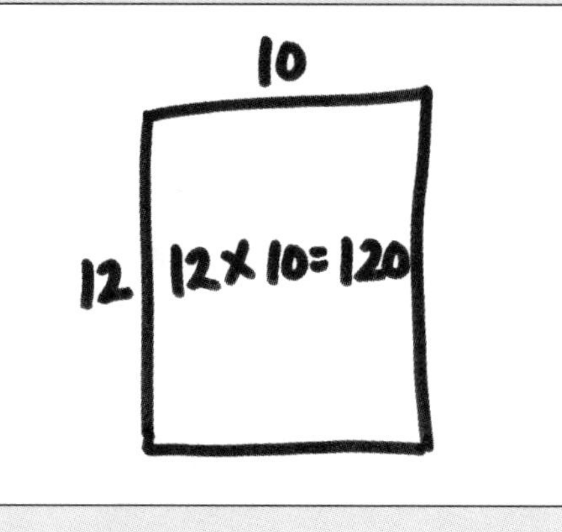

open array shows 12 times 10, which is the first step in this strategy. How could we add on to our array to show the entire strategy?

Munira: We could keep going and add on another 12 times 10.

Mr. Tavana: What would that look like, Munira?

Munira: You go 10 more over up here. *(Using her finger, she traces on the easel to show what it would look like to extend the line across. Mr. Tavana hands her the pen and she begins drawing—starting at the top and labeling it 10.)* And then go down and connect to the first array. That's another 12 times 10 equals 120, like from right here in the strategy *(pointing to the second recorded 12 × 10 = 120 in the solution on the strategy poster and then labeling the new 12 × 10 portion of the open array. [See Figure 6.10.]*

Figure 6.10 Munira has added on to the array to keep track of the multiplying-up strategy for division.

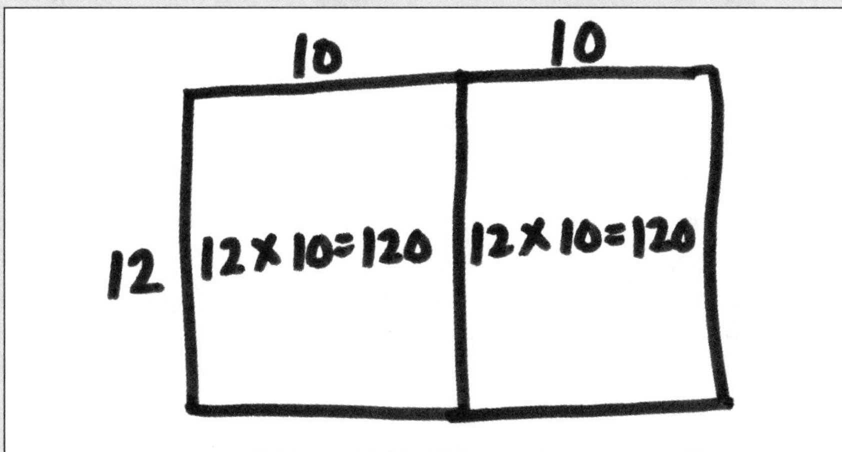

Mr. Tavana: Okay, Munira, thank you for helping us. Let's pause to think about what we are seeing in this open array. As you look at our open array, I want you to think about where we can see each part of the strategy. Where is the 12 times 10, 12 times 10, 120 plus 120 equals 240? *(Pointing to the poster and then giving wait time.)* Can you turn to your neighbor and take turns pointing to where each of these parts of the strategy can be seen in our open array? *(Students turn and talk and Mr. Tavana listens in to select a few students to share.)* I was listening in as you talked to your neighbor and I wanted to ask Jaddis to share what he was saying. Jaddis was pointing to the strategy poster and the open array poster. Jaddis, will you come up and point for us?

Jaddis: *(Standing between the strategy poster and the open array.)* Here is the first 12 times 10 *(pointing to the left-hand side of the open array)*, and all of this in here, this chunk *(sliding his hand over the 12 × 10 area on the left side)* shows 120.

Mr. Tavana: Let's stop there for a moment, because Jaddis is telling us something important. In this open array on the left side, we see 12 down and 10 across, and together this whole area shows 120. This chunk, as Jaddis called it. In our problem we knew that we were dividing by 12, but we didn't know how many groups of 12 we would have in 240. We are seeing that we can build out in ten groups of 12, something we all know, to try to get all the way to 240. Okay, keep going, Jaddis.

Jaddis: So then we did that same thing again. We made another 10 groups of 12 here, another chunk *(pointing to the open array on the right side of poster)*, and then *(moving his hand from left to right across the array)* all this area, a chunk of 120 and another chunk of 120, gets us out to 240.

Mr. Tavana: Did you just see the way Jaddis moved his hand all the way across the open array? Jaddis, do that again. *(Jaddis runs his hand across the first and second groups of 120.)* We knew we were making groups of 12, and we made 10 groups and then another 10 groups, and that built out our 240. This is an open array, so we don't draw all of the lines inside, but if we did, we could see that here is one group of 12, here is another group of 12 *(tracing his finger down in columns of 12)*, and in this first portion of the open array there would be 10 columns of 12 and in this second portion there would be another 10 columns of 12.

Mr. Tavana notices one student, Nicholas, has reached for Unifix cubes and is starting to build stacks of 12 cubes. He is keeping an eye on Nicholas, because if he is building 20 stacks of 12, it could illustrate all the parts of an array that would resemble more of a filled-in array. This visual may be handy in bridging to the idea of an open array.

Mr. Tavana: So, what would it look like to label the 240 in our open array? Faysal?

Faysal: This whole part here, all of this in here *(moving her hand around on the poster to cover the two sections of 12 × 10)*.

Mr. Tavana: All of this in here. Let's show that. All together *(using a red pen, draws around the perimeter of the array and then labels the total)* we have 240. Now, where is our answer? What is 240 divided by 12? Noelia, I see you pointing to our poster. Where is our answer?

Noelia: *(Jumping up.)* It's right there. *(Pointing to the 10 and the 10 on top of the array.)*

Mr. Tavana: *(Turning to the class.)* Do you agree with Noelia's idea? And why?

Amara: I agree, because down here, this is the 12 *(pointing to the side of the array)*, and then inside, that's how much *(pointing to the 240)*, and so then up here *(pointing to the 10 and 10)*, this is the other number. And there is 10 and 10, so that is 20.

Mr. Tavana: Okay, let's label that 10 and 10 makes 20 at the top. *(He adds on to the drawing. [See Figure 6.11.]* So we are saying that 10 groups of 12 *(tracing his hand across the left side of the open array)* and then 10 more groups of 12 *(tracing across both sides)*, or 20 groups of 12, is 240.

Figure 6.11 The array is annotated to show where the dividend and the quotient appear for the division problem 240 ÷ 12.

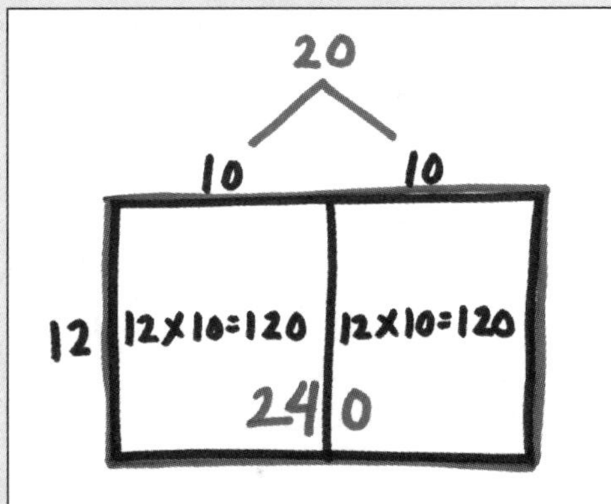

Mr. Tavana: What would a number sentence look like for 240 divided by 12?

Miski: Um, it would be like 240 divided by 12 is 20.

Mr. Tavana: Okay, Miski, will you label that for us? *(Miski writes the equation beneath the open array. [See Figure 6.12.])*

Figure 6.12 The array is labeled with this division equation.

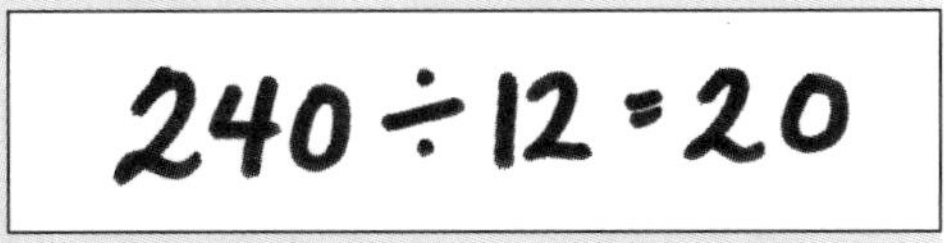

$$240 \div 12 = 20$$

Mr. Tavana: Today we used a tool, an open array, to help us make sense of this division strategy. We have used an open array before, but today we are using the open array in a different way. When we use what we know about multiplication to divide, we are making chunks, like Jaddis said, to build up to our total, and an open array can help us see what those chunks look like. Making drawings of our thinking can help us really understand what we are doing when we use a strategy.

The lesson concludes, and Mr. Tavana is still keeping an eye on Nicholas, who is indeed building 20 stacks of 12 Unifix cubes. When Nicholas finishes, Mr. Tavana will check in with him to hear about his thinking and will likely use the array with cubes that Nicholas builds to connect the open array to a three-dimensional model.

Summary and Reflection Questions: When Do I Want to Have a Define and Clarify Discussion?

The three vignettes in this chapter show how different mathematical objects can become the focus of a Define and Clarify discussion. Explicit conversations about how and when to use these tools and concepts accurately are important components of making mathematical work accessible and meaningful to students. Some of these discussions arose out of confusions or stumbling blocks that students faced, which we'll discuss further with the next chapter's Troubleshoot and Revise discussion structure.

Before you read on, reflect on the questions below, which are specific to tools and are inspired by questions that Victoria Jacobs and Julie Kusiak raise in their article "Got Tools? Exploring Children's Use of Mathematics Tools During Problem Solving" (2006):

- In your next unit, what are the key mathematical tools and concepts that students will be using: new terms, notations, representations, or tools? Which of these might be new to students? How might a Define and Clarify discussion support students to make the most out of the new tool or concept?
- Some students, especially upper-grade students, may be resistant to using concrete tools or objects, because they associate them with younger grades. What can you do to convince your students that using tools is not only acceptable but also an important mathematical strategy?

CHAPTER 7

TARGETED DISCUSSION: TROUBLESHOOT AND REVISE

Working through confusion and building on partial understanding plays an important role in learning mathematics. As the Common Core State Standards for Mathematical Practice remind us, mathematically proficient students "make sense of problems and persevere in solving them" (2012, 6). Engaging in discussions about puzzling mathematics allows a teacher and his or her students to take stock of what makes sense and work through stumbling blocks together. However, this is delicate work, because thinking through errors and revising your thinking publicly can be challenging—especially in mathematics, where there is a perception that "smart" students solve problems quickly and always get the right answer. The norms for learning from errors, which are nurtured in the classroom, are vital in making this type of discussion successful.

A Troubleshoot and Revise discussion can be initiated by the teacher or by one or more students. In either case, the teacher or student has noticed something is awry and seeks the collective engagement of the class to figure out what needs to be revised. The way Megan Staples and Melissa Colonis (2007) think about managing discussion of "wrong" answers is helpful. They find wrong answers to be a "catalyst" for discussions and point out that the discussion is more than an opportunity to just correct the wrong answer; it can "help the student and the class extend the idea that had been presented and continue to develop a viable solution collaboratively" (259). Therefore, a Troubleshoot and Revise discussion can be initiated for a variety of reasons. Students might recognize that they have partial understandings and are stuck. They might notice that a strategy they used, which seemed to make sense, resulted in an answer different from that of their classmates. The teacher might also notice a misunderstanding that is bubbling up and worthy of attention.

As we think about how teachers can use errors as opportunities for advancing mathematical thinking, we will also think carefully about how teachers can treat students as sense makers and find the logic in students' partial understandings as they facilitate mathematically productive and socially supportive discussions. We want students to know that thoughtful mathematicians voice their confusions; thinking collaboratively through errors can help everyone better understand the mathematics. We want to frame mistakes as "desirable contributions" (Staples 2008, 52).

The two vignettes in this chapter explore different ways of structuring a Troubleshoot and Revise discussion. In the first vignette, third-grade teacher Mr. Barber initiates a discussion about a misconception that arose when his students were finding fractions of a set. In the second vignette, one of Ms. Simpson's fourth graders requests a consultation from his peers when he becomes confused by a true/false number sentence.

Third Graders Troubleshoot Finding Fourths Versus Fours: "What's the Logic in This Thinking?" "What's Getting Mixed Up?"

Mr. Barber's third graders have been working with different ways of conceptualizing fractions. They are in the midst of finding fractions of a set: finding halves, fourths, and fifths. Mr. Barber ends many of his lessons with an exit ticket, asking students to show their understanding of the day's focal concept on a notecard that they leave with him. This allows him to get a quick read on how his students are using an idea.

When he reviewed the exit tickets after one lesson, he noticed that some students were confusing partitioning a set of objects into fourths with making groups of four. He uses the Troubleshoot and Revise planning template to plan a whole-class discussion about this issue (see Figure 7.1; a blank version of this planning template is provided in Appendix F).

Figure 7.1 Mr. Barber's Planning Template for a Troubleshoot and Revise Discussion about Finding Fourths Versus Fours

Troubleshoot and Revise
What is the confusion or misunderstanding we will discuss and revise? Finding fractions of a set—revise a strategy that confuses "how many in a group?" with "how many groups?" Students are making groups of 4 instead of seeing the whole group divided into four equal groups. Use problem context of Mr. Barber's cookies from exit slip: Mr. Barber had 24 cookies. If he gave three-fourths of all the cookies to his friend, how many cookies did he give his friend?
What is the insight I'd like students to understand? The set of 24 was divided into four equal groups, resulting in fourths. Mr. Barber gave three of those fourths to his friend.
Problem context, diagrams, or questions that might be useful to use during the discussion • Show a solution in which 24 cookies were put into groups of 4, resulting in 6 groups: oooo oooo oooo oooo oooo oooo • Why might someone think like this to solve the problem? • How does it not match the problem situation? • What would the problem say if it were asking you to make groups of 4? (Students might say: He gave 4 cookies to each friend.) • What does the problem say to help you know that it's asking you to make 4 groups? • What does "fourths" mean?
Exit ticket What's the difference between putting something in groups of four and making fourths?

Mr. Barber: A few days ago we were talking about fractions of a set. After our discussion, you filled out an exit ticket to help me know how you were thinking about this idea. The problem on the exit ticket looked like this. *(Pointing to the board, where the exit ticket problem is displayed. [See Figure 7.2.])*

Mr. Barber: Do you remember thinking about this problem? Let's read the problem again with partners to make sure we all remember. Partner 1, will you read the problem aloud? And partner 2, please repeat the problem. *(Students, who are all sitting on the carpet, turn to face their partners and read and repeat the problem.)*

Figure 7.2 The Exit Ticket Problem

Mr. Barber had 24 cookies. If he gave three-fourths of all the cookies to his friend, how many cookies did he give his friend?

Mr. Barber uses turn-and-talk here in a unique way. His students are assigned partners, and he often asks partner 1 or partner 2 to talk about certain things during turn-and-talks.

Mr. Barber: Okay, I can hear we have all read the problem. Today I want to have another discussion about this problem to help us understand what it means to find a fraction of a set. When I was looking at your thinking on the exit slips, I saw several students use a strategy that needs revision. In our class, we talk about our strategies, and when there is something we don't completely understand, we help each other think about how to revise our ideas. *(Pointing to the poster where he has already drawn the strategy of dividing 24 cookies into groups of 4. [See Figure 7.3.])* Today, as we discuss the strategy I've drawn on this poster, I am going to ask us to think about two things. First, we are going to talk about the logic in this solution. Or, why does it make

Figure 7.3 Mr. Barber prepared this poster to show the problem and the strategy that needs revision.

Mr. Barber had 24 cookies. If he gave 3 fourths to his friend, how much did he give to his friend?

0000|0000|0000|0000|

0000|0000|

He gave 12 to his friend.

sense that someone might try to solve this problem in this way? Second, we are going to talk about two ideas that are getting mixed up. Let's start by thinking about the logic in this thinking, or why someone would think about this problem in this way. Take a moment to look at the solution on this poster, and place a thumb on your chest when you have an idea about the logic in this thinking.

During the wait time, Mr. Barber is watching the students think, and he is also using the wait time to think himself. He is thinking about how he is setting up this discussion. He is working hard to bring to life the idea that all children are sense makers and that their ideas are valued. This is especially delicate when the discussion focuses on a partial understanding. By starting with finding the logic in an approach, he is nurturing the idea that there are reasons why a solution contains a mistake.

Mr. Barber: I can see that many people have ideas. I think we should begin by chatting with our partners about this. Please turn and talk to your partner.

Mr. Barber listens in and overhears students talking about the picture on the poster, saying things like, "There are four cookies in each group," "This strategy shows four in a group," and "Yeah, there are four in a group, but we have to find four groups." He decides to invite some of these students to share their ideas.

Mr. Barber: I am going to invite Laloni and Rafi to share what they were noticing.

Laloni: Um, Rafi and I were saying that the problem says that he gave three-*fourths* away, and we see fours in this picture.

Rafi: *(Standing up to point to the poster and circling the four cookies in each group with her finger. [See Figure 7.4.])* These right here; here are the fours.

Mr. Barber: *(Turning to the class.)* Do you hear what Laloni and Rafi are noticing about what makes sense in this thinking? Did you hear the way Laloni remembered that this problem is about putting the cookies into fourths and how Rafi is seeing four cookies in each group? Can you add on to what they are noticing? Neeku? And let's stay focused on what makes sense about why someone would think this way.

Figure 7.4 This portion of the poster shows four cookies in each group.

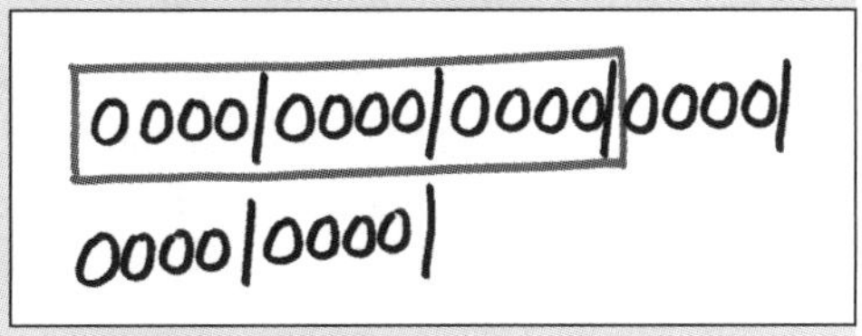

Neeku: It makes sense that someone might want to put four in a group because we are finding fourths, but . . . is it okay if we move to what someone using this solution might be confused about?

Mr. Barber: *(Glancing to the class to seek their approval before moving on, he nods.)* Yes, I think it is okay. What are you thinking about, Neeku?

Mr. Barber knows that beginning the discussion with a focus on the logic of the solution treats the students using this strategy as sense makers. Seeing that this solution puts four cookies in a group begins by honoring what children using this strategy understand about grouping and division. He now senses the logic is visible, and it is okay to move to make sense of what is confusing.

Neeku: It is kind of tricky, because you are supposed to put the cookies into four groups . . . um . . .

Mr. Barber: Here are some cubes to help you, or you can draw on the bottom of our poster to show your thinking.

Neeku: *(Taking the pen and approaching the poster.)* You see there are four in a group here? This mathematician put four in each group, four in a group. But what we really need is four groups.

Mr. Barber: Who can repeat what Neeku just said about the thinking of mathematicians who used this strategy? Rocio? Then, others, you can just jump in and repeat.

Rocio: There are four in each group, but we need four groups.

Ralph: The person who used this did not put them in four groups; he or she put four in a group.

Landen: There are four in a group, but we need four groups. It is, like, how many groups, not how many in a group.

Mr. Barber: We are hearing a difference between how many cookies to put in a group and how many groups of cookies to make. Let's look back at our story. *If he gave three-fourths to his friend.* Let's stop there and read that part again. Mr. Barber had 24 cookies. If he gave three-fourths to his friend. What does the part about fourths mean? How could we use the ideas that Neeku, Rocio, Ralph, and Landen shared to make sense of what it means to make fourths? Jordan? You can use the cubes or the poster if that is helpful.

Jordan: *(Grabbing a handful of cubes and then quickly counting out 24.)* If these are your cookies, you have to put them into four groups.

Mr. Barber: Four groups, or fourths. Can we watch you make those four groups?

Figure 7.5 Jordan makes four groups of cubes on the carpet.

Jordan: *(Doling out the cubes into four piles. [See Figure 7.5.])* One, 2, 3, 4, 5, 6, 7, 8 . . .

Mr. Barber: As you pass out those cookies into the four groups, Jordan, can you tell us why you are doing that for this problem?

Mr. Barber is asking Jordan to explain his thinking for two reasons. One is to hear the idea of making four groups again and underscore why that makes sense for this problem context. Another reason is to practice asking children questions when their solution is correct, not just incorrect. Mr. Barber frames ideas that are not fully mathematically correct as learning opportunities and also treats correct solutions as opportunities to ask students questions. Students can come to think a teacher's questions mean there is something wrong with their ideas. The importance of a teacher pressing students to engage in this type of dialogue when solutions are correct will help children practice sharing when their answers are correct as well as incorrect.

Jordan: I'm making four piles because the problem says he gave three-fourths away. So first we have to make four groups. Once I make these four piles, the cookies will be in fourths. Like the whole group of cookies *(Mr. Barber inserts, "The 24 cookies")* will be in fourths, or four groups.

Eileen: Oh, wait! Wait, something is making sense to me now.

Mr. Barber: Eileen, what is happening for you?

Eileen: I was someone who used this strategy and I thought I needed to put four cookies in a group, but now I hear that I was really supposed to make four groups of cookies. Like this. *(Grabbing the pen and drawing on the poster.)* Here are four circles for groups and I'm putting a cookie in each group. (See Figure 7.6.)

Mr. Barber: Eileen, that is really exciting thinking you're doing! Smart mathematicians do just what you are doing—they continue thinking about problems and revise their thinking. In our classroom when you get more information and you want to change your thinking, you say, "I want to revise my thinking." Does anyone else want to revise their thinking like Eileen?

Figure 7.6 Here the poster shows four groups of cookies.

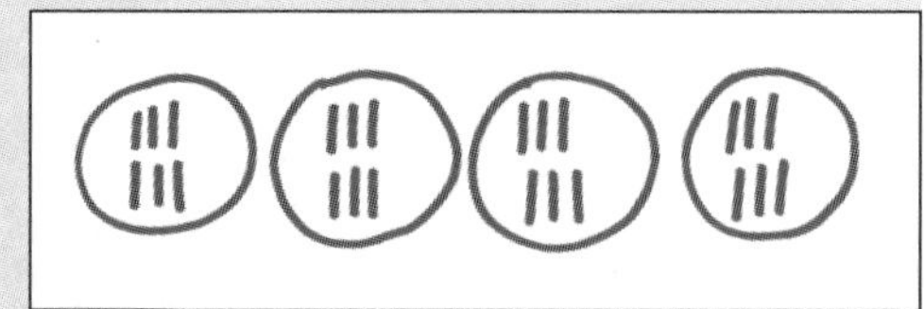

Mr. Barber is supporting students in knowing that changing your idea when you have more information is a good thing to do, and he is explicitly telling children what you say when this happens.

Ruth: I do. I used this strategy too and I thought it was about making four in a group, but it is about making four groups like Jordan and Eileen did.

The class goes on to solve the rest of the story by figuring out how many cookies constitute three-fourths. Mr. Barber emphasizes the idea that everyone has a greater sense of fractions because of their opportunity to collectively think about this challenging concept together, and that without the investigation into this confusion, they would not all have the deeper understanding they now have about fractions of a set. The discussion ends with an affirmation of the way the class is able to make sense of this solution together and underscores the norms in this classroom for talking through misconceptions, the power of collaborative thinking, persisting through puzzling ideas, and revising ideas as new insights are developed. To check where each student is, Mr. Barber uses an exit ticket to collect students' ideas by asking them to answer the question, "What's the difference between putting something in groups of four versus finding fourths?"

"I Don't See Why This Statement Is False": Fourth Graders Troubleshoot and Revise Their Ideas About Relational Thinking

Ms. Simpson has noticed that her fourth graders are using ideas about the way multiplication behaves as they work on division strategies. In multiplication, students can break up either factor in order to create subproducts that can be combined to find the product. For example, when multiplying 75×14, students can break up the 75 or the 14 (or both).

$$75 \times 14 = (75 \times 10) + (75 \times 4)$$
or
$$75 \times 14 = (70 \times 14) + (5 \times 14)$$

This approach doesn't work in division, unless the divisor and dividend are both changed proportionally. When Ms. Simpson's class moves to a unit on division, she often uses true/false equations to challenge students to think relationally—to evaluate how the expressions are related on either side of the equal sign when determining whether a statement is true or false (Carpenter, Franke, and Levi 2003). When she sees one of her students, Jason, working hard to make sense of a particular true/false statement during morning work, Ms. Simpson asks him if he would like to troubleshoot his puzzlement with his class (see Figure 7.7). He thinks it would be a good idea. He has seen other classmates do

Figure 7.7 Ms. Simpson has a consultation with Jason to see if he would like a troubleshooting discussion with his classmates.

this type of sharing and knows that all those minds working together can be really powerful. Since this situation has come up rather spontaneously, and it is in the midst of class, Ms. Simpson quickly sketches out her ideas on a planning template (see Figure 7.8).

Ms. Simpson has to plan slightly differently for a troubleshooting discussion that begins with a student sharing. She has to ready herself to slow down

Figure 7.8 Ms. Simpson's Planning Template for a Troubleshoot and Revise Discussion About Relational Thinking

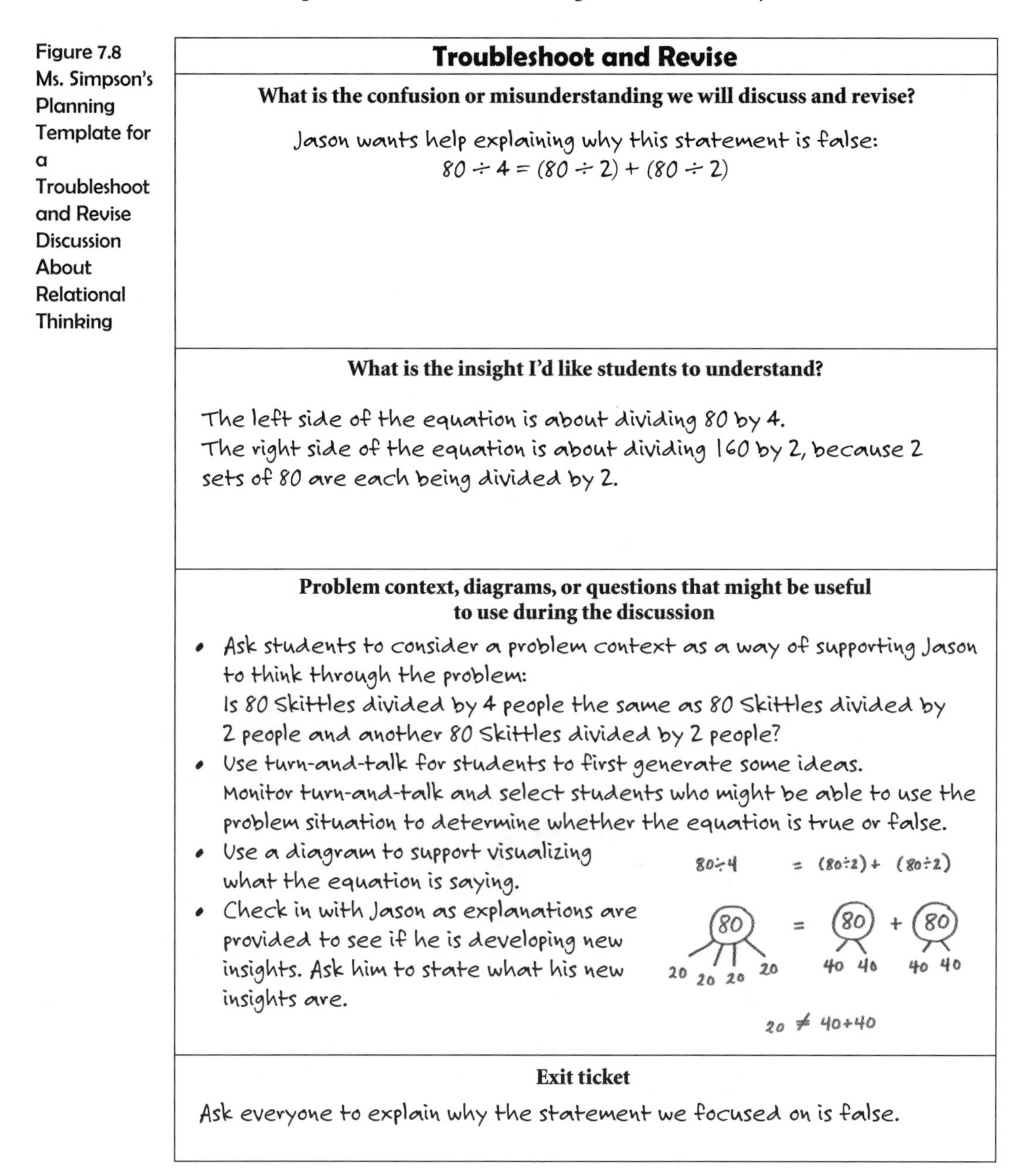

Troubleshoot and Revise

What is the confusion or misunderstanding we will discuss and revise?

Jason wants help explaining why this statement is false:
$80 \div 4 = (80 \div 2) + (80 \div 2)$

What is the insight I'd like students to understand?

The left side of the equation is about dividing 80 by 4.
The right side of the equation is about dividing 160 by 2, because 2 sets of 80 are each being divided by 2.

Problem context, diagrams, or questions that might be useful to use during the discussion

- Ask students to consider a problem context as a way of supporting Jason to think through the problem:
  Is 80 Skittles divided by 4 people the same as 80 Skittles divided by 2 people and another 80 Skittles divided by 2 people?
- Use turn-and-talk for students to first generate some ideas.
  Monitor turn-and-talk and select students who might be able to use the problem situation to determine whether the equation is true or false.
- Use a diagram to support visualizing what the equation is saying.
- Check in with Jason as explanations are provided to see if he is developing new insights. Ask him to state what his new insights are.

Exit ticket

Ask everyone to explain why the statement we focused on is false.

the conversation and really help the student who initiates the troubleshooting develop some new insights. But she also wants to be sure that the whole class benefits from the discussion.

Ms. Simpson: Okay, everyone, Jason would like our help with something he's finding quite perplexing. Remember, our job is to try to understand what Jason's questions are and then to help him think through the puzzle. We need to be generous with one another and be willing to look at this puzzle in more than one way. And you might find that you share Jason's puzzle, which is just great.

Ms. Simpson points to a poster she has made to remind students about ways of asking questions and stating ideas during a Troubleshoot and Revise discussion (see Figure 7.9). Ms. Simpson likes to remind her listeners how to think about the discussion that is about to take place.

Jason: So, I was working on this true/false problem that we got in our morning work and I thought it was true, but then Damien showed me that if you work out the numbers it can't be true. So now, I'm kind of confused.

Ms. Simpson: Let's put the true/false number sentence up so everyone can look at the one you're talking about.

$80 \div 4 = (80 \div 2) + (80 \div 2)$

Figure 7.9 This poster provides sentence stems students can use during troubleshooting discussions.

Troubleshooting

For asking my classmates to help me think:

I am not sure about something and I want to ask for ideas.

Can you help me understand why ______?

I want to revise my thinking.

For helping my classmates think:

Can you tell us more about what is confusing you?

What part feels the most confusing to you?

What do you understand about ______?

What do you know that can help you think about this?

Ms. Simpson: I'm wondering if someone can ask Jason a question.

Ms. Simpson prompts her students to ask Jason a question. She wants to help them learn how to ask questions of one another, so that she is not the only person asking questions.

Simon: Why did you think it was true?

Jason: I thought it was true because you're cutting 4 in half. It's 80 divided by 2, and then it's another 80 divided by 2. Because 2 plus 2 equals 4.

Preston: I thought it was true too. Because if you switch it around, it's 80 divided by 2 and 80 divided by 2 equals 80 divided 4. And 2 plus 2 equals 4. And the 80 stays the same.

Ms. Simpson sees a few other students nod in agreement. She often finds a Troubleshoot and Revise discussion supports more than just one student.

Ms. Simpson: Okay, so Jason, it's great that we are bringing this to the class for troubleshooting because it looks like some other people thought this was true as well. Let's be sure we understand the logic you were using to think through this. Who has another question for Jason?

Angela: *(Looking at the sentence stems on Ms. Simpson's poster.)* What do you understand about the 80?

Jason: I think the 80 is just what you're dividing.

Craig: What is the most confusing to you?

Jason: Well, I know that 2 plus 2 is 4, so I just don't understand why it's not true.

Ms. Simpson: So, can everyone turn to his or her partner and check in with one another? Do you understand what Jason is asking us?

Partners talk, pointing to the true/false equation as they talk. Ms. Simpson listens in on many of the conversations and hears that the class is focused on what Jason is saying.

Ms. Simpson: I think we're ready to give Jason some ideas to think about. What I heard Jason say is that he thought this statement had to be true because he saw that 4 was split up into 2 and 2 on the right side of the equal sign and the 80 stayed the same. Sometimes it helps us to think about a story problem as we think through a true/false statement. So, let me put a story problem around this. Is 80 Skittles divided by 4 children the same amount as 80 Skittles divided by 2 children and 80 Skittles divided by 2 children? Think about that.

Ms. Simpson decides to revoice Jason's question for the class herself. She also decides to offer a story problem context for the class to use, because contextualizing the quantities into a concrete situation can support relational thinking. She's not sure her students would necessarily think to generate a problem context themselves. Again, Ms. Simpson offers important thinking time for students to ponder the problem.

Min: What I think might help Jason is that if you have 80 Skittles and you do 80 divided by 2, then you already split up all the Skittles. You can't do it again, because all the Skittles are already gone. You can't change the divisor. You can only change the dividend.

Ms. Simpson: Jason, you look like you're not sure about what she said. Can you repeat what she said?

Jason: She said that you can't change the divisor, the 4.

Ms. Simpson: Right, that's part of what she said. Are you wondering why she said you can't change the divisor?

Jason: Yeah.

Ms. Simpson: Great. You can ask her to tell us again, and everyone, as you're listening, think about what Min is saying.

Ms. Simpson noticed that Jason picked up on the last part of what Min said; however, "You can't change the divisor" doesn't quite capture all of what is happening in this statement. She wants to slow this part of the conversation down and orient students to one another's ideas. She does this by asking Jason to hear from Min again.

Min: Because that's how many kids there are.

Ms. Simpson: And say again what were you saying about the 80 Skittles?

Min: If you split the 80 Skittles between the 2 people, then you already split all the Skittles and you can't split them again.

Ms. Simpson: So what do you think, Jason, about what she said? She said if you've split 80 Skittles between 2 people, you've used them up and you can't split them again. What do you think about that?

Jason: I'm beginning to think that it's false.

Ms. Simpson: So you're beginning to wonder. Akaya, what did you want to add?

Akaya: Can I come up? *(Ms. Simpson nods to her to come to the board.)* If you look at it, 80 divided by 4 is 20. Eighty divided by 2 is 40, and we can see that 20 is not the same as 40 + 40. *(She writes the inequality below the original one. [See Figure 7.10.])*

Ms. Simpson: So Akaya is showing us that when we do the computation, we can see

Figure 7.10 This class poster shows that 20 is not the same as 40 + 40.

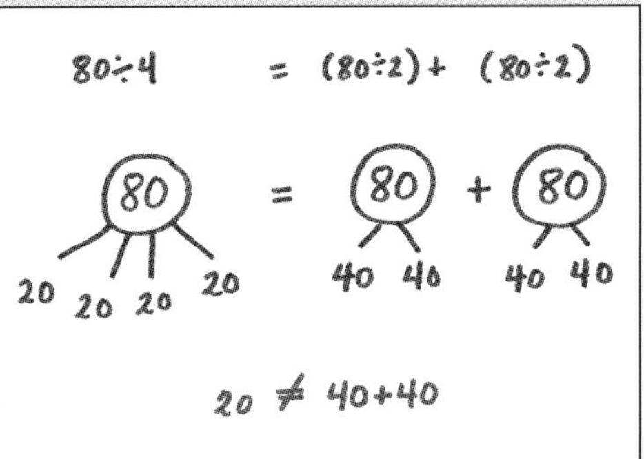

that the equation is not true. Let's try to connect that to the reasons Min is giving us too, about using up all the Skittles. Let's also add a picture of what this means. Let's draw a bag of Skittles. In this bag of Skittles, how many Skittles are there? Everyone?

Everyone together: Eighty!

Ms. Simpson: And 80 divided by 4 tells us that we need 4 equal portions—so let me show that in the picture. *(Ms. Simpson adds to the poster by drawing a bag of Skittles divided up into 4 equal portions.)*

Now, with your partner, think about what the picture that goes on this side of the equation is going to look like *(pointing to the right-hand side of the poster)*. You can use your whiteboards to do this.

Ms. Simpson uses a turn-and-talk to again engage the whole class in making sense of the true/false statement. Because this Troubleshoot and Revise discussion was initiated by Jason, she moves to where he is talking with his partner to see the picture that he and his partner Addie are working on. She wants to support his choice of taking a risk in front of his classmates by bringing his confusion to the whole class. After seeing that he is making progress in figuring out what was confusing to him, she asks him to come up and finish the picture on the easel so that everyone can see a full representation of this equation.

Ms. Simpson: *(Signaling the class to come back together.)* Five, 4, 3, 2, 1. Let me invite Jason to share the picture that goes with this side of the equation *(pointing to the open space on the right-hand side of the poster)*.

Jason: Addie and I worked on this picture, and I think I see what Min is saying. On this other side, it has 80 divided by 2 and then another 80 divided by 2. So I have to draw two bags of Skittles. What Min said makes sense. If I split up 80 for 2 people, like for me and Damien, then I don't really have any more Skittles left. But this side says I have 2 bags of 80 Skittles. So really, it's like I have 160 Skittles on this side, not 80. *(Jason finishes the picture. [See Figure 7.11.])*

Ms. Simpson: This is a great time to check in with one another and see if we are agreeing with the new thinking that Jason is sharing with us. Before we turn to talk, can you show Jason a thumbs-up if you are agreeing with his new thinking? (See Figure 7.12.)

After the pair share, Ms. Simpson asks everyone to write their thinking on an exit ticket. It's always helpful to get a read on the whole class. She has learned not to rely on just one discussion to solidify important ideas. She

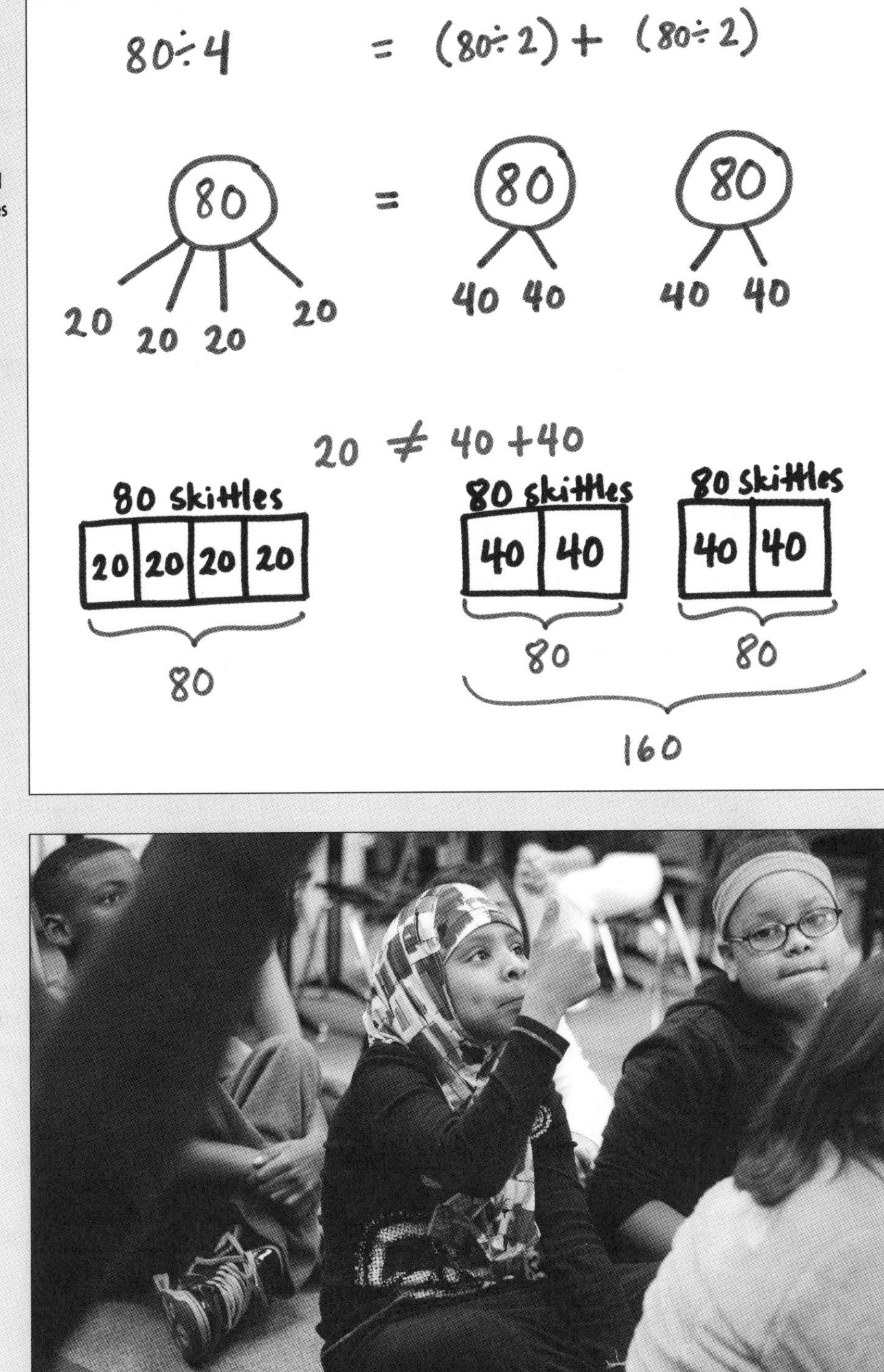

Figure 7.11 The poster eventually shows the understanding reached by Jason and his classmates about why $80 \div 4 = (80 \div 2) + (80 \div 2)$ is false.

Figure 7.12 Students show Jason they understand and agree with his new thinking.

knows that individual time for reflection and trying to put a new idea into one's own words is an important part of the learning process. She thinks the students have made progress today and sees the beginnings of many more explorations: When can you change the divisor in division? How might students explain why $80 \div 4 = 40 \div 2$?

Summary and Reflection Questions: When Do I Want to Have a Troubleshoot and Revise Discussion?

We find the *Consultancy Protocol*, designed for use in Critical Friends Groups and developed by Gene Thompson-Grove and National School Reform Faculty, to be very helpful in thinking about how a teacher or student can initiate a discussion that works to troubleshoot and revise a mathematical idea or strategy. This protocol explains that "a Consultancy is a structured process for helping an individual or a team think more expansively about a particular, concrete dilemma. Outside perspective is critical to this protocol working effectively; therefore, some of the participants in the group must be people who do not share the presenter's specific dilemma at that time" (1). Similarly, a Troubleshoot and Revise discussion is an opportunity for a student or group of students to think aloud together about mathematics that may be puzzling and, using the ideas of others, engage in collaborative sense making. Sometimes a confusion is minimal and may not warrant a group discussion. Other times, the confusion is greater, such as when students are mixing up important mathematical understandings or when an error is prevalent among the students in a class. A targeted discussion is useful in slowing down the conversation to uncover the confusion and bring new understanding. You may want to have a Troubleshoot and Revise discussion in these situations:

- You observe several students in your class grappling with an idea, and you think other students could help clarify the confusion.
- A student comes to you with an idea he or she is willing to put in front of the class, and you believe the class has the resources to support the student in thinking through the idea.
- You want to support norms for revising one's thinking.

Before you go on to the next chapter, reflect on these questions:

1. What worries me and excites me about facilitating Troubleshoot and Revise discussions with my students?
2. What do I think about the role of mistakes and confusion in learning mathematics with understanding?
3. How were mistakes and confusions framed when I was a learner of mathematics? How do I want to frame mistakes and confusions in my classroom?

CHAPTER 8

CONCLUSION: REFLECTING AND LEARNING

The vignettes in this book are not idealized portrayals of what students *might* be able to attain. They describe what students and teachers are capable of accomplishing together. We hope you've found them to be useful as you plan how to start your school year, how to foster joy for doing mathematics, how to navigate through your curricular resources, and how to support students to be successful in mathematics.

Do I Really Have Time for These Types of Discussions?

You may be wondering, "Do I really have time for these types of targeted discussions?" And you've probably already guessed our answer to this question! Most mathematics texts direct teachers to have discussions with their students. The teacher's guide might list questions to ask students but may not provide much explicit direction about what the goal of the discussion should be. For example, the text might say, "Have students compare their strategies" or "Discuss how to use an array." And according to the Common Core Standards for Mathematical Practice, students are expected to make sense of each other's ideas and to reason through the viability of an argument. We hope we have provided some guidance on how to structure discussions to attain particular goals. We think that when teachers take the time to facilitate sustained discussions, students will learn mathematics in ways that will stick.

When Discussions Are Student Centered, What Is My Role as the Teacher?

We can see in the vignettes that discussions thrive when students take on active roles and their ideas are at the heart of the talk. But when discussions are student centered, teachers often wonder about their role. While the teacher in student-centered discussions may appear more like a "guide on the side" than a "sage on the stage," the teacher's role in leading productive mathematical discussions cannot be minimized. For example, remember in Chapter 7 when Mr. Barber and his students were engaged in a Troubleshoot and Revise discussion in order to make sense of how students were dividing up the 24 cookies? In this vignette, students were actively making sense of and revising a common strategy that contained an error. During this discussion, Mr. Barber made many important moves and decisions in order to reveal the logic in the misconception and make sense of fractions of a set. If you glance back through the vignette, you may notice some of his actions: he decided when students needed think time, he listened in during a turn-and-talk in order to select and sequence which ideas were shared in the whole group, he revoiced important ideas that emerged and invited students to repeat, he oriented students back to the problem context and narrowed upon key mathematical ideas, he provided cubes to help act out the story, and he pointed out the importance of persisting through confusions and the value in examining errors.

Reading the vignettes with an eye for the moves and decisions the teacher makes will help underscore the critical role a teacher plays in fostering productive mathematical discussions. In every vignette, the teacher is working hard to monitor what students are doing and understanding, who is engaged and not, and who needs more time or different supports to stay with the discussion. The teacher makes intentional choices in the mathematical objects that are used in the discussions, how to enter and close math talk, what to do to assess the success of the discussion, and the next steps to continue to build understanding and fluency. You may have noted additional things that a teacher is doing in these discussions. His or her role is anything but passive!

How Do Students Feel About Participating in These Discussions?

We wrote this book from the teacher's perspective, giving you insight into what the teacher is thinking and trying to accomplish. But how do students feel about participating in these discussions? Over the course of several years, as we have worked closely with teachers to learn how to foster productive classroom discussions, we have always had an eye out for how students feel about listening to and sharing ideas. After all, these discussions can be intellectually and socially risky. We want students to know that they have good ideas, but ideas in formation don't always come out in perfectly comprehensible ways, and some ideas need to be revised. How we set and maintain norms for engaging in classroom participation is important. When we asked the students we described in this book how they felt about participating in discussions and what they listen for, we heard comments like the following:

- When I share my thinking about what I'm confused about, it helps me revise my ideas. We say, "I want to revise my thinking." I don't feel ashamed because I know a lot of people revise their thinking.
- Sometimes I forget my idea when I'm listening to another person, but it comes back.
- When I'm listening to my classmates, I think about how they got their answer. If I don't understand how they got it, I ask them to explain it again.
- When my classmates repeat my ideas, I'm thinking about how my idea can help other students learn. When I hear my idea repeated again, I can learn from that, too.
- During a turn-and-talk I'm thinking about what my partner said and how their math idea connects with mine.

These types of comments can help you know whether students are adopting the norms that you want them to. To give you insight about how your students are feeling about participating in discussions, it might be useful to survey your students regularly about their perspectives. Their thoughts and feelings can provide good launching points in classroom meetings as they monitor how they are doing as a group. You might like to ask students to rate their feelings with statements like the following:

I like to share my math strategies in class.
most of the time **some** of the time **a little** bit **never**

My classmates can learn from my math strategies.
most of the time **some** of the time **a little** bit **never**

Listening to other students' math strategies helps me.
most of the time **some** of the time **a little** bit **never**

You might also like to pose some open-ended questions like the following:

1. What does it mean to be good at math?
2. What's it like for you to listen to other people's strategies during math class?
3. How do you feel about being called on to share your thinking?
4. How do you feel about revising your thinking?

With younger students, we have found that drawing and writing or talking about pictures can provide great insight for teachers. A prompt like, "Draw a picture of yourself in math class and tell me about it," can open up dialogue about being listeners and sharers.

How Can I Plan for Open and Targeted Discussions?

When you are making plans for a new unit, think about when you might use the discussion structures described in this book. Begin by listing the strategies that students are supposed to learn by the end of the unit. For example, in one second-grade unit on addition, students are expected to learn the following:

- Combining tens and ones (e.g., $67 + 34 = 60 + 30 + 7 + 4$)
- Incrementally adding on tens and then ones to a quantity (e.g., $67 + 34 = 67 + 30 + 4$)
- Regrouping tens when adding more than ten ones

Once you have listed the focal strategies in the unit, you will have identified what strategies might emerge in open strategy sharing. Thinking further about how the strategies are related to one another might lead you to plan out a few Compare and Connect discussions.

You can plan to use other discussion structures in this book by noting the following:

1. What kinds of justifications might students need to generate during this unit?
2. Are there times when one strategy might be more efficient than another?
3. What new mathematical objects (e.g., vocabulary, tools, representations, notation) will my students be using?
4. What errors might my students make?

Your responses to each of these questions and consideration of when they might be occurring in the unit will help you see openings for the discussion structures described in this book. Ask yourself what lessons in the unit lend themselves to one or more of the open or targeted discussions. You might not use each of these discussion structures in each unit. But it might help you to anticipate ahead of time which might be particularly relevant.

Resources

In the appendixes, you'll find blank planning templates for each of the discussion structures (Appendixes A through F). Many of the lessons featured in this book are routine activities that can be used as warm-ups or lessons that you can seamlessly integrate into your math units at almost any grade level. In Appendixes G, H, and I, we've included protocols for Counting Collections, Number Talks, and Quick Images to help you with your planning. We have also included a list of online video clips which illustrate different topics covered in our book and an annotated list of our favorite books on teaching math in the elementary grades (Appendix J).

Thank you for taking this journey with us. We know that your own experimentation with these discussion structures will generate new ideas and support you and your students to experience mathematics as a rich and rewarding discipline.

APPENDIX

Appendix A: Planning Template for Open Strategy Sharing Discussion

Open Strategy Sharing		
Problem to pose		
Why I chose this problem		
Opening the lesson		
How might my students solve this problem?	**Who solved it this way?**	**Who should share today?**
Notes to myself about what I'm looking for		
Other strategies that emerged during the lesson		
Closing the lesson		

Intentional Talk: How to Structure and Lead Productive Mathematical Discussions by Elham Kazemi and Allison Hintz. Copyright © 2014. Stenhouse Publishers.

Appendix B: Planning Template for Compare and Connect Discussion

<table>
<tr><th colspan="2">Compare and Connect</th></tr>
<tr><th>Strategy 1</th><th>Strategy 2</th></tr>
<tr><td></td><td></td></tr>
<tr><td colspan="2">What connections are important for students to notice?</td></tr>
<tr><th colspan="2">Supporting Students' Thinking</th></tr>
<tr><th>What students might notice</th><th>How I might respond to support their thinking</th></tr>
<tr><td></td><td></td></tr>
<tr><td></td><td></td></tr>
<tr><td></td><td></td></tr>
<tr><td colspan="2">What is the key mathematical idea I want to highlight?</td></tr>
</table>

Intentional Talk: How to Structure and Lead Productive Mathematical Discussions by Elham Kazemi and Allison Hintz. Copyright © 2014. Stenhouse Publishers.

Appendix C: Planning Template for Why? Let's Justify Discussion

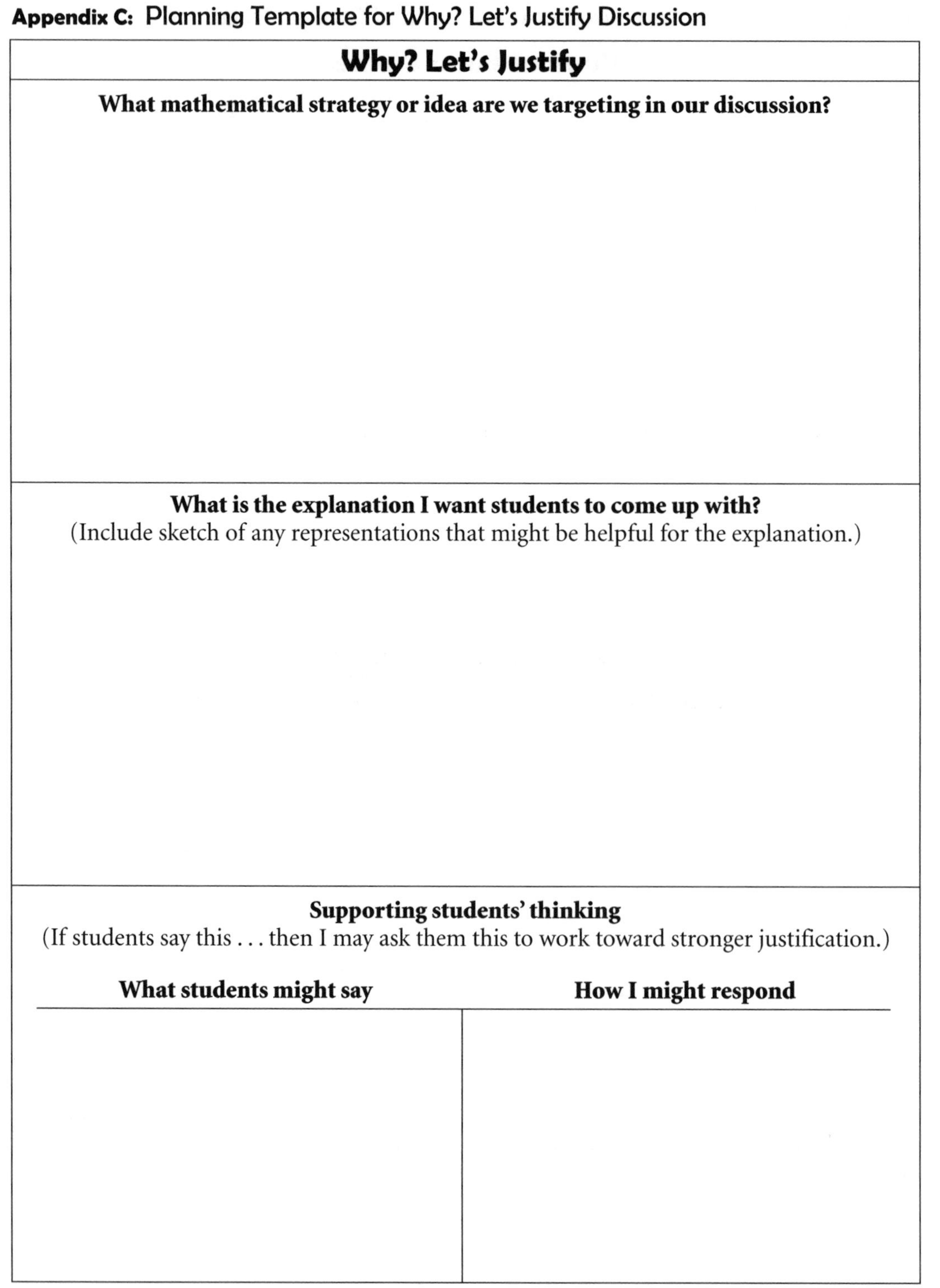

Why? Let's Justify

What mathematical strategy or idea are we targeting in our discussion?

What is the explanation I want students to come up with?
(Include sketch of any representations that might be helpful for the explanation.)

Supporting students' thinking
(If students say this . . . then I may ask them this to work toward stronger justification.)

What students might say	How I might respond

Intentional Talk: How to Structure and Lead Productive Mathematical Discussions by Elham Kazemi and Allison Hintz. Copyright © 2014. Stenhouse Publishers.

Appendix D: Planning Template for What's Best and Why? Discussion

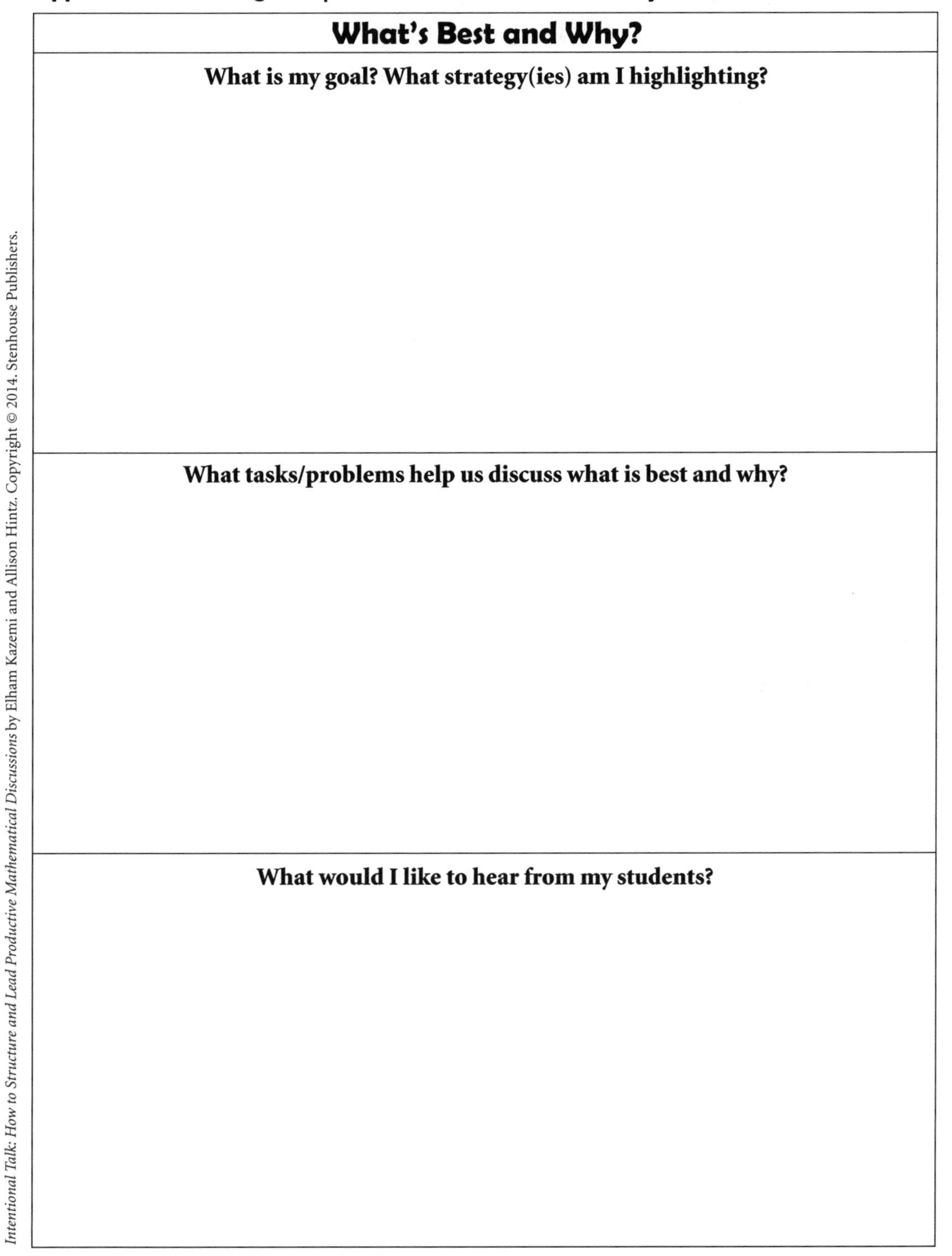

What's Best and Why?
What is my goal? What strategy(ies) am I highlighting?
What tasks/problems help us discuss what is best and why?
What would I like to hear from my students?

Intentional Talk: How to Structure and Lead Productive Mathematical Discussions by Elham Kazemi and Allison Hintz. Copyright © 2014. Stenhouse Publishers.

Appendix E: Planning Template for Define and Clarify Discussion

Define and Clarify
What new tool, representation, symbol, or vocabulary are we targeting in our discussion? Is this new to the students or are they using it in a new way?
What problem or task are we working on? How will I support meaning making? What partial understandings might arise?

Intentional Talk: How to Structure and Lead Productive Mathematical Discussions by Elham Kazemi and Allison Hintz. Copyright © 2014. Stenhouse Publishers.

Appendix F: Planning Template for Troubleshoot and Revise Discussion

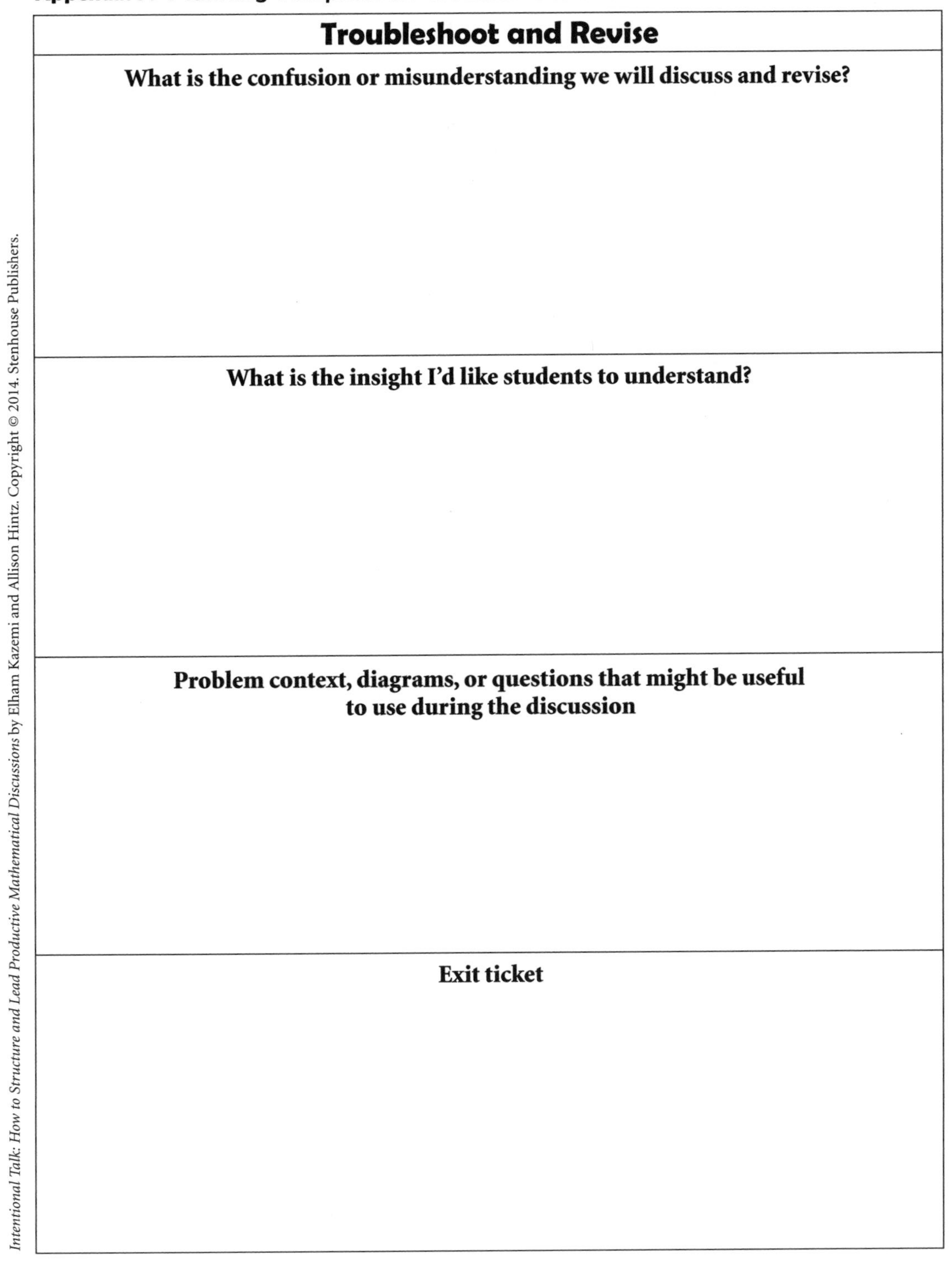

Troubleshoot and Revise
What is the confusion or misunderstanding we will discuss and revise?
What is the insight I'd like students to understand?
Problem context, diagrams, or questions that might be useful to use during the discussion
Exit ticket

Intentional Talk: How to Structure and Lead Productive Mathematical Discussions by Elham Kazemi and Allison Hintz. Copyright © 2014. Stenhouse Publishers.

Appendix G: Counting Collections

Getting Started
Create 13 or more collections. • Gather a variety of items to count. Examples: bottle caps, pasta, birthday candles, stones, glass marbles, hair ties, playing cards, game pieces, buttons, beads, craft sticks, foam stickers, pom-poms, game pieces, paper clips, crayons, tiles, cubes, pattern blocks.  • For experienced counters, gather collections that come in packages that can't be opened (boxes of 100 paperclips, 12 pencils, 8 crayons, mini boxes of candy, reams of paper, etc.). • Put each collection in a plastic zippered bag or plastic container. • The size of your collections will vary with your students. For example: Kindergarten collections might range from 25 in September to 150 or more later in the year. First graders may begin with counts of 50 to 100 and later to count 200 as they transition to counting by tens and ones. Second and third graders may begin counting 100 to 150 objects by ones. They will transition to counting large numbers (300+) of objects by tens and ones and counting sets of various sizes (e.g., boxes of 8 crayons).
Prepare other materials. • Gather a collection of cups, bowls, egg cartons, or other small containers for students to use to organize their counts. • Have hundreds charts available for younger students. • Print recording sheets for students. • Print anecdotal record sheets for teachers.

Instructional Decisions to Consider	Notes
What size count is appropriate for my students? Which students are ready to count sets of objects?	
How will I group my students? • Individuals or pairs? • Based on social skills or math skills?	

Created by Lakeridge Elementary School together with the University of Washington, 2012. Adapted from Kern Schwerdtfeger, Julie, and Angela Chan. 2007. "Counting Collections." *Teaching Children Mathematics* 13(7): 356–361. Counting Collections was developed by Megan Franke, PhD, UCLA.

Intentional Talk: How to Structure and Lead Productive Mathematical Discussions by Elham Kazemi and Allison Hintz. Copyright © 2014. Stenhouse Publishers.

Appendix G: Counting Collections (continued)

	Notes
How often will we count collections? How much time will we spend for each session?	
What are the social goals for the lesson? Examples: • Count with my partner. (Make decisions about where to work, how to count, how to record.) • Stay on task.	
What are the mathematical goals for the lesson? Examples: • Keep track of the items counted. • Record efficiently. (Represent with tallies, X's, or circles, rather than drawings of the actual items being counted.) • Record in a way that shows how you counted. • Count efficiently. (Use groups to count.) • Decompose numbers to count. (Count by tens and twos rather than twelves.)	
What do I want to pay attention to as I observe students? How will I ensure that I observe all students over time?	
Social Challenges	
• Students may have difficulty staying on task. • Students may have difficulty working with a partner or sharing the task.	
Math Challenges	
• Students may get distracted by the items themselves. They may sort objects by color or size before they begin to count. • Students misstep at predictable or consistent numbers (decades 29 . . . 30; century marks 399 . . . 400; counting by tens 100, 110, 120). • Students can count higher than they can record, especially if they are counting by ones. • Students may not record the way they counted. (For example, they count by tens but record ones.)	

Created by Lakeridge Elementary School together with the University of Washington, 2012. Adapted from Kern Schwerdtfeger, Julie, and Angela Chan. 2007. "Counting Collections." *Teaching Children Mathematics* 13(7): 356–361. Counting Collections was developed by Megan Franke, PhD, UCLA.

Intentional Talk: How to Structure and Lead Productive Mathematical Discussions by Elham Kazemi and Allison Hintz. Copyright © 2014. Stenhouse Publishers.

Appendix G: Counting Collections (continued)

Lesson Planner	Lesson Notes
Mathematical Goal	
Social Goal	
Launch (5 min.) When you first begin counting collections you may want to model these things: • How to work with a partner • Ways to keep track of your count • Ways you might record In later lessons, share student strategies (counting, grouping, or recording) from the last count.	
As students count . . . • Try not to provide teacher directions about how to count. Let students develop their own strategies that make sense to them. • Be open to the various ways that students group objects • Ask students to show you how they counted. • Name a child's counting strategy and encourage other students to give various strategies a try. ("I see you put 5 beads in a cup and then counted up by fives.") • If students finish early, they can get another bag to count or can try to count their objects a different way.	
As you walk around . . . • Take notes using the anecdotal record sheet. • Are students able to keep track of what is being counted? How are students keeping track? *"How do you know which ones you've counted and which ones you haven't counted?"*	

Created by Lakeridge Elementary School together with the University of Washington, 2012. Adapted from Kern Schwerdtfeger, Julie, and Angela Chan. 2007. "Counting Collections." *Teaching Children Mathematics* 13(7): 356–361. Counting Collections was developed by Megan Franke, PhD, UCLA.

Intentional Talk: How to Structure and Lead Productive Mathematical Discussions by Elham Kazemi and Allison Hintz. Copyright © 2014. Stenhouse Publishers.

Appendix G: Counting Collections (continued)

	Lesson Notes
• Are students working together? *"It looks like the two of you are using different strategies. Do you have a plan for how you will add your totals together?"* • Are students beginning to group objects? If so, how? Do they combine groups to make larger groups? *"Why did you decide to put these into ______?"* (e.g., cups of 5, 10, or 50.) • Can students count by ones? Tens? Tens and ones? *"How many cups did it take to get to 150? If you made another set of 10 cups how many would you have?"* • What strategies are students using to count by sets? *"What made this collection tricky to count?"*	
Summary / Debrief Share student strategies based on the mathematical or social goals that you wanted to highlight. (Preselect one or two student strategies to share.) Strategies might include these: • Strategies for keeping track of how many we counted • Strategies for grouping • Strategies for counting sets of objects	
Celebrate student successes!	

Created by Lakeridge Elementary School together with the University of Washington, 2012. Adapted from Kern Schwerdtfeger, Julie, and Angela Chan. 2007. "Counting Collections." *Teaching Children Mathematics* 13(7): 356–361. Counting Collections was developed by Megan Franke, PhD, UCLA.

Intentional Talk: How to Structure and Lead Productive Mathematical Discussions by Elham Kazemi and Allison Hintz. Copyright © 2014. Stenhouse Publishers.

Appendix H: Number Talks: Posing a Set (or String) of Related Problems

This instructional activity asks teachers to engage a group of students in a focused exploration of computational strategies or approaches and ideas about operations. This task is designed to highlight efficient computation strategies (often but not necessarily done mentally) and an understanding of the meaning of mathematical operations. Each problem in the string is designed to build on the thinking used to solve previous problems: there are explicit connections and relationships among the problems. The task requires that teachers choose a sequence of related problems that would be productive and accessible for their students, yet engage them in learning. It also requires that teachers manage engaging all students in participation, responding to student comments and questions, and choosing problems that are likely to develop certain strategies or big ideas that the teacher knows are important. The task is designed as one that can be used routinely in a way that is productive for students. It is also designed so that teachers can take advantage of and build upon many mathematical ideas that emerge. The task can be a springboard for the upcoming mathematical work in the lesson.

Step 1: Choose a purposeful sequence of related problems.

- Be sure that you have thoughtfully chosen or created a string with a specific mathematical purpose. What is the string designed to highlight? What relationships or strategies do you want participants to notice?

Step 2: Introduce the task to students and anticipate the flow/pacing.

- Keeping your purpose in mind will help you decide when to delve into and when to gloss over particular problems and/or strategies. For example, you may want to tell participants you expect them to "just know" the first problem in a string (although this is not always the case!). Also, if someone shares a rather complicated strategy that does not match your goals, you may choose not to ask that student a lot of probing questions. In contrast, if someone has shared the strategy you'd like students to focus on, slow the conversation down by asking someone else to restate the strategy.
- Decide what management device you want students to use to signal that they have their answer. Be sure to consider how your management routine conveys messages about competence, status, competition, speed, and so on.

Step 3: Pose the first problem.

- Start with a problem that you know the kids will find easy.
- Get answer(s) from kids.
- Decide if you want to link the answer to a particular representation such as an array or a number line.
- Decide if you want to be in charge of the representation or have the kids create or direct you in creating the representation.
- Listen to student response and decide if clarification, elaboration, or explanation is needed. If a student shares a strategy you want to highlight, decide how much elaboration, revoicing, and rephrasing you want to do or request that other students do.

Intentional Talk: How to Structure and Lead Productive Mathematical Discussions by Elham Kazemi and Allison Hintz. Copyright © 2014. Stenhouse Publishers.

Appendix H: Number Talks: Posing a Set (or String) of Related Problems (continued)

- Decide if you want to request a different strategy or if you want to ask students to comment on or build upon the current strategy.
- Decide how to use other student voices to explain mathematical reasoning.
- Decide how to record students' mathematical reasoning.

Step 4: Pose the second problem.

- Think about how to keep the problems of the string visible to the students if you also have been recording their strategies.
- Request answer(s) from student(s).
- Decide how you want a student to link his or her answer back to the representation. Request the student to describe how he or she got an answer(s).
- Decide how you want students to treat different answers and strategies shared thus far. Do you want to comment or have students comment on the similarities or differences? Do you want to make an explicit link to how the strategies used on previous problems might support solving this problem?

Step 5: Pose the remaining problems.

- Pose each problem one at a time and consider all ideas from steps 3 and 4.
- Note: If the last problem in the string is an application of the ideas that the string is designed to focus attention on, explicitly tell students you are posing a new problem. For example: *"Now I'm going to pose a new problem with different numbers. See if the work we've just done with ______ idea helps you get the answer for this one."*

Step 6: Highlight the big ideas and close the task.

- Discuss the specific strategy that this string was designed to address. Work with students to make connections among the problems within the string. Make explicit the mathematical strategy or concept that this string highlighted.
- Decide whether it is necessary to pose another similar problem in which students might be able to use the strategy just discussed and highlighted in the string.

Challenges That Might Occur

- Children offer incorrect responses.
- Many children seem not to be participating.
- You ask for any connections among the problems and get no response.
- Children are not seeing connections among problems; they are not using previous problems in the string to solve the harder problems that come nearer the end of the string.

Adapted from activities described in Fosnot and Dolk (2001).

Intentional Talk: How to Structure and Lead Productive Mathematical Discussions by Elham Kazemi and Allison Hintz. Copyright © 2014. Stenhouse Publishers.

Appendix I: Quick Images

This instructional activity asks teachers to engage a group of students in quickly visualizing quantities and discussing how they organized and subitized quantities in order to count the total in the picture. The task requires that teachers choose an image that would be productive and accessible for their students to count when quickly flashed for them, yet engage them in learning. It also requires that teachers manage participation and respond to student comments and questions.*

Step 1: Choose and prepare a Quick Image.

- Consider what mathematical ideas you would like to highlight with the image(s) you have selected.
- Consider how you will "flash" the image for students: on an overhead, with a document camera, as a poster, with a context, and so on.
- Consider whether you want a sequence of images (two to three can be completed in a ten-minute session) or just one.

Step 2: Introduce the task to students.

- Talk to students about what the task is and clarify instructions.
- Be sure to remind students not to call out their answer.
  I'm going to show you a picture of ______ for three seconds and then cover it up. I want you to keep your eyes on the picture and try to figure out how many ______ there are.

Step 3: Flash an image for three seconds.

Show the image for as close to three seconds as possible. It's important not to show it for too long, as students might try to count by ones rather than visualize and subitize the numbers.

Step 4: Students determine the answer.

- Give students a few moments to consider the total number of items in the image.
- You may want to have students draw the image on paper (or another tool) to help them visualize and determine the answer.
- It may be helpful to have students give you a visual sign to show that they have an idea about the total so that you know to move on to the next step.

Step 5: Flash the image again, for revision.

- Show the image again for three seconds for students to check their thinking and revise their thinking if necessary.
- Allow a few moments (after showing the image a second time) for students to consider how they know their answer is correct or how they may want to revise their drawing or their thinking. You might ask students: "How can you prove to me that your answer is the same as the number of items in the picture?" or "How are you organizing the items in the picture to count them all together?"
- You might allow a few moments for students to talk together in pairs to discuss their ideas.

Intentional Talk: How to Structure and Lead Productive Mathematical Discussions by Elham Kazemi and Allison Hintz. Copyright © 2014. Stenhouse Publishers.

Appendix I: Quick Images (continued)

Step 6: Show the image a third and final time.

This time, leave the image visible so that all students can check their answer (and drawing) and revise their thinking if necessary.

Step 7: Discuss the mental images students formed.

- Now you want to know what students noticed about the total number in the image and the ways in which they organized or subitized the parts. This is where a lot of mathematical ideas will emerge for you to ask questions about and build upon.
- Ask, "What answers do we have?"
- List all the answers. If there's more than one answer, you can say, "It looks like we have several ideas. As we share, let's see which of these ideas we need to revise."
- Ask, "How did you count to find the total? How did you see the ______?" (Dots or picture.)
- Or you may want to focus in on a particular mathematical idea. For example, "How many groups of four did you see in the picture?" and "How might counting by the groups of four be faster or more efficient than counting by ones?"
- Choose one thing you want to follow up on—either a pattern shared or a question about particular content. You don't want this to go on and on.

Step 8: Repeat steps 3–6 for additional image(s).

Step 9: Close the task.

You want to bring this task to a close. You can do this by repeating some of the ideas students shared or a response they gave to your questions—but in doing so your goal is to repeat and highlight an important mathematical idea for your students. The image(s) should still be visible so you can use it/them to point out what you are talking about.

* Protocol adapted from Technical Education Research Centers, *Investigations in Numbers, Data, and Space* curriculum.

Intentional Talk: How to Structure and Lead Productive Mathematical Discussions by Elham Kazemi and Allison Hintz. Copyright © 2014. Stenhouse Publishers.

Appendix J: Resources for Further Reading or Illustration

Video Resources

Supporting Student Learning

Visit https://www.teachingchannel.org/videos/student-participation-strategy for a short video highlighting key moves teachers can make to engage students in discussion.

Visit https://www.teachingchannel.org/videos/students-acknowledging-other-ideas to see how a teacher supports students to listen to one another by acknowledging who authored an idea.

Visit https://www.teachingchannel.org/videos/teacher-assessment-strategy to see how a teacher uses exit cards at the end of a lesson to monitor for student learning.

Visit http://www.edutopia.org/math-social-activity-cooperative-learning-video to see the way a teacher helps students come up with a set of social agreements for their mathematics class.

Instructional Activities and Discussions

Some of the vignettes in the book occur within routine instructional activities that can be good vehicles through which to orchestrate open or targeted discussions.

Visit https://www.teachingchannel.org/videos/skip-counting-with-kindergarteners to see Counting Collections with kindergartners.

Visit https://www.teachingchannel.org/videos/counting-collections-lesson to see Counting Collections with third graders.

Visit https://www.teachingchannel.org/videos/multiplication-division-in-the-core to see open strategy sharing within a counting and mental math activity.

Visit http://vimeo.com/66205198 to see an example of a Why? Let's Justify discussion in a second-grade classroom as students try to explain the commutative property of addition.

Visit http://vimeo.com/66202272 to see an example of a Define and Clarify discussion as second graders work to create a model for a separating situation.

Books

Carpenter, Thomas P., Elizabeth Fennema, Megan L. Franke, Linda Levi, and Susan B. Empson. 1999. *Children's Mathematics: Cognitively Guided Instruction.* Portsmouth, NH: Heinemann. A new version of this book will be out in 2014. Use this book to guide your understanding of how children's thinking in number and operations in the elementary grades develops. You will find many ideas to guide Strategy Sharing and Compare and Connect discussions.

Carpenter, Thomas P., Megan L. Franke, and Linda Levi. 2003. *Thinking Mathematically: Integrating Arithmetic and Algebra in Elementary School.* Portsmouth, NH: Heinemann. This book is an excellent source of true/false equations that can help you work on Why? Let's Justify targeted discussions.

Intentional Talk: How to Structure and Lead Productive Mathematical Discussions by Elham Kazemi and Allison Hintz. Copyright © 2014. Stenhouse Publishers.

Appendix J: Resources for Further Reading or Illustration (continued)

Chapin, Suzanne H., Catherine O'Connor, and Nancy C. Anderson. 2009. *Classroom Discussions: Using Math Talk to Help Students Learn.* 2nd edition. Sausalito, CA: Math Solutions.
This book shows how to support students to learn the discussion expectations in your classroom, provides many vignettes to see the talk moves in action, and has practical lesson ideas for your classroom.

Empson, Susan B., and Linda Levi. 2011. *Extending Children's Mathematics: Fractions & Decimals: Innovations in Cognitively Guided Instruction.* Portsmouth, NH: Heinemann.
This book is an excellent source of problems to support children's understanding of fractions and decimals and to inform the goals you set for open or targeted sharing.

Featherstone, Helen, Sandra Crespo, Lisa M. Jilk, Joy A. Oslund, Amy N. Parks, and Marcy B. Wood. 2011. *Smarter Together! Collaboration and Equity in the Elementary Math Classroom.* Reston, VA: National Council of Teachers of Mathematics.
This book provides a vision for how to support students to work together and show all students that their ideas are valued.

Parrish, Susan. (2010). *Number Talks.* Sausalito, CA: Math Solutions.
A source of sequenced computation problems to work on particular strategies. This book provides great fodder for What's Best and Why? discussions. Many video clips that accompany this book provide ideas for how to encourage students to participate and how to teach them to carefully use representations to make ideas clear to listeners.

Russell, Susan Jo, Deborah Schifter, and Virginia Bastable, 2011. *Connecting Arithmetic to Algebra: Strategies for Building Algebraic Thinking in the Elementary Grades.* Portsmouth, NH: Heinemann.
This book contains many examples of how to support students to generate strong justifications to develop their understanding of number and the behavior of the operations.

Shumway, Jessica. 2011. *Number Sense Routines: Building Numerical Literacy Every Day in Grades K–3.* Portland, ME: Stenhouse.
In this book you will find lots of idea for tasks that can build students' understanding of number, and routine activities to use regularly throughout the year.

Smith, Margaret S., and Mary Kay Stein, 2011. *5 Practices for Orchestrating Productive Mathematics Discussions.* Reston, VA: National Council of Teachers of Mathematics.
The five practices for orchestrating discussions in this book are enormously helpful in planning for discussions in general.

Storeygard, Judy, ed., 2009. *My Kids Can: Making Math Accessible to All Learners, K–5.* Portsmouth, NH: Heinemann.
This book contains many examples of productive classroom discussions and describes how to engage a broad range of learners, particularly students with special needs. One of the many video clips that accompany this book provides a great example of a teacher asking students how they use the tens frame to help them count an arrangement of dots, which provides an example of Define and Clarify.

Intentional Talk: How to Structure and Lead Productive Mathematical Discussions by Elham Kazemi and Allison Hintz. Copyright © 2014. Stenhouse Publishers.

REFERENCES

Aguirre, Julia, Karen Mayfield-Ingram, and Danny B. Martin. 2013. *The Impact of Identity in K–8 Mathematics: Rethinking Equity-Based Practice.* Reston, VA: National Council of Teachers of Mathematics.

Carpenter, Thomas P., Megan L. Franke, and Linda Levi. 2003. *Thinking Mathematically: Integrating Arithmetic and Algebra in Elementary School.* Portsmouth, NH: Heinemann.

Chapin, Suzanne H., Catherine O'Connor, and Nancy C. Anderson. 2009. *Classroom Discussions: Using Math Talk to Help Students Learn.* 2nd edition. Sausalito, CA: Math Solutions.

Common Core State Standards Initiative. 2012. "Standards for Mathematical Practice." http://www.corestandards.org/assets/CCSSI_Math%20Standards.pdf.

Delpit, Lisa. 2012. *"Multiplication Is for White People": Raising Expectations for Other People's Children.* New York: New Press.

Featherstone, Helen, Sandra Crespo, Lisa M. Jilk, Joy A. Oslund, Amy N. Parks, and Marcy B. Wood. 2011. *Smarter Together! Collaboration and Equity in the Elementary Math Classroom.* Reston, VA: National Council of Teachers of Mathematics.

Fosnot, Catherine T., and Maarten Dolk. 2001. *Constructing Number Sense: Addition and Subtraction.* Portsmouth, NH: Heinemann.

Hiebert, James, Thomas P. Carpenter, Elizabeth Fennema, Karen C. Fuson, Diana Wearne, Hanlie Murray, Alwyn Olivier, and Piet Human. 1997. *Making Sense: Teaching and Learning Mathematics with Understanding.* Portsmouth, NH: Heinemann.

Jacobs, Victoria R., and Julie Kusiak. 2006. "Got Tools? Exploring Children's Use of Math Tools During Problem Solving." *Teaching Children Mathematics* 12(9): 470–477.

Lannin, John K., Amy B. Ellis, and Rebekah Elliott. 2011. *Developing Essential Understanding of Mathematical Reasoning for Teaching Mathematics in Prekindergarten–Grade 8.* Reston, VA: National Council of Teachers of Mathematics.

Michaels, Sarah, Mary Catherine O'Connor, and Megan Williams Hall. 2010. *Accountable Talk Sourcebook: For Classroom Conversations That Work.* University of Pittsburgh: Institute for Learning. ifl.lrdc.pitt.edu/ifl/index.php/download/index/ats/.

Paley, Vivian. G. 1986. "On Listening to What the Children Say." *Harvard Educational Review* 56(2): 122–131.

Parrish, Sherry. 2010. *Number Talks: Helping Children Build Mental Math and Computation Strategies.* Sausalito, CA: Math Solutions.

Russell, Susan Jo. 1999. "Mathematical Reasoning in the Elementary Grades." In *Developing Mathematical Reasoning in Grades K–12.* 1999 NCTM Yearbook, ed. L. Stiff. Reston, VA: National Council of Teachers of Mathematics.

Russell, Susan Jo, Deborah Schifter, and Virginia Bastable. 2011. *Connecting Arithmetic to Algebra: Strategies for Building Algebraic Thinking in the Elementary Grades.* Portsmouth, NH: Heinemann.

Schwerdtfeger, Julie K., and Angela Chan. 2007. "Counting Collections." *Teaching Children Mathematics* 13(7): 356–361.

Shumway, Jessica F., 2011. *Number Sense Routines: Building Numerical Literacy Every Day in Grades K–3.* Portland, ME: Stenhouse.

Smith, Margaret S., and Mary Kay Stein. 2011. *5 Practices for Orchestrating Productive Mathematics Discussions.* Reston, VA: National Council of Teachers of Mathematics.

Staples, Megan. 2008. "Promoting Student Collaboration in a Detracked, Heterogeneous Secondary Mathematics Classroom." *Journal of Mathematics Teacher Education* 11(5): 349–371.

Staples, Megan, and Melissa Colonis. 2007. "Making the Most of Mathematical Discussions." *Mathematics Teacher* 101(4): 257–261.

Storeygard, Judy, ed. 2009. *My Kids Can: Making Math Accessible to All Learners, K–5.* Porstmouth, NH: Heinemann.

Technical Education Research Centers. n.d. *Investigations in Numbers, Data, and Space* curriculum. http://investigations.terc.edu/.

Thompson-Grove, Gene, and National School Reform Faculty. n.d. *Consultancy Protocol.* National School Reform Faculty. http://www.nsrfharmony.org/protocol/doc/consultancy.pdf.

INDEX

Page numbers followed by an *f* indicate figures.